Advertising that Sells

A Primer For Product Managers

By
Miner Raymond

BLACK
ROSE
PUBLISHING

Black Rose Publishing Co., Inc.

Published by Black Rose, Inc.
1420 E. McMillan
Cincinnati, Ohio 45206

Design and Illustrations by Tom Dusterberg

Type set by Pagemakers; Cincinnati, Ohio

Library of Congress Catalogue Number 89-086005

ISBN 0-9624575-0-7

To My Beloved Editor

ACKNOWLEDGEMENTS

I am vastly indebted to all those from whom I've so freely borrowed knowledge and ideas: Ran West, Mark Wiseman, David Ogilvy, Rosser Reeves, Fred Cammann, Gordon Webber, Alan Sidnam, Ed Lotspeich, Tom Cadden, Barney Carr, George Cooney, Dick Bryan, Bill Craig, Dick Ward, Bill Graf and Jim Broering. I am also indebted to the thousands of Brand Managers I've had in seminars — who have taught me fully as much as I've imparted to them. Finally, profound thanks to my associates in Miner Raymond Associates: Fran Furtner, Larry Haggart, Ron Harding — and most especially Deborah Fette, who typed this manuscript so many times with such patience and grace.

Table of Contents

HOW
AND WHY
THIS BOOK
GOT
WRITTEN

Over the past 40 years, I've worked on somewhere around 25,000 commercials. That's a two-ton truckload of experience.

The first thousand or so commercials I wrote, as an advertising agency copywriter, copy chief, and creative director. The other 24,000 I either created, helped in the creation of, produced, supervised, hauled into being, or beneficially messed around with. In the course of a lifetime in television, I either innovated or helped in the development of a number of execution techniques which continue to be "rediscovered" by agency people in each succeeding decade — just as if they had never existed before.

There really is nothing new in the basic forms of human communication. The same principles apply today as applied when the only cable in America was the coaxial, which first linked TV stations to form networks.

So far as I know, the first image, or "lifestyle," television advertising was developed for Zest in the mid-1950s. Zest also inaugurated the first attempt to preselect a television commercial's target audience by means of the style of the music used, a pounding track by a vocal group called the Hi-Los. That music was so new and disturbing it nearly brought a premature end to a promising career by getting me fired from the World's Largest Television Advertiser. (We all survived — the track, the Hi-Los, and I.) Zest also introduced the first quick-cut, jingle-driven commercial; and incorporated the first commercial use of "dutch angles," a technique lifted unashamedly by Marshall Stone from German expressionistic films of the 1930s. Those were the exhilarating days when Ed Mahoney,

Ray Lind, Hoyt Allen, Gordon Webber, and the creatives and remarkably astute and patient account people at Benton & Bowles would try anything, if it showed the least amount of promise.

In like fashion, I worked on TV's first testimonial commercials, Cheer epics devised by Hanley Norins, an inordinately gifted creative director at Young & Rubicam. Subsequently, it fell to me to write up the executional principles to be observed in producing effective testimonial-commercial advertising. I codified those how-to's for broadscale application within Procter & Gamble. And, at a time when P&G's slice-of-life technique was first brought to full flower by Jack Hirschboeck and a number of other skilled writers at Burnett (with a similar cadre at the Biow agency, which was subsequently folded into Grey), I laid out the principles on slice-of-life in an early 1960s memo — which, I'm told, still exists in desks around the country . . . yellowed copies in clear violation of anybody's file retention program.

The lineal antecedent of Charmin's Mr. Whipple, Charley, Dash's washer repairman, Bounty's Rosie, and Folger's Mrs. Olsen was a butler for Hudepohl Beer on a half-hour musical variety show, produced in Cincinnati 40 years ago. Ran West of Stockton, West, Burkhart was the agency creator; I helped write the commercials and produced the show. (As I recall, the total production budget for a fully-funded half-hour band, singer, and act extravaganza, starring Betty Clooney, was $850 per episode!)

In addition, I devised and sold Procter & Gamble on many of the methods of buying production (including the still-employed cost-plus-fixed-fee system) that have over the decades saved that company many dozens, if not hundreds, of millions of dollars.

So Why Write A Book?

An associate manager in the general advertising department of the World's Largest Television Advertiser is well-counseled to adopt a profile lower than an annelid's hernia. Procter & Gamble staffers are expected to come up with helpful analyses and useful points of view for the organization paying their salaries; and it's only reasonable that staff people should be happy to remain among the faceless hordes.

On the other hand, since 1980 I have been operating Miner Raymond Associates, Inc. — currently the world's largest and most comprehensive commercial and communications consulting firm. Many of the principles outlined in this book were first circulated as newsletters to our valued clients and prospects, who have been kind enough to say they find them helpful and applicable. Now seems like a good time to give those notions broader circulation.

In the late days of this century, advertising appears to be floundering directionless through a creative Sahara. Agency work forces (and services to clients) shrink as revenues grow; but nobody's getting rich, and no advertising seems to be improving. Therefore, now seems ap-

2

propriate to articulate some simple but tested principles which Product Managers — and those who work for, with, above, and through them — can adopt easily and apply beneficially to their businesses.

One of the principles you will see running as a leitmotif through this book is that advertising really doesn't change much over the years. Essentially, there are — just as there have been from the beginning — two basic forms of advertising.

There's the product/benefit-oriented school — highly-structured, carefully planned and thought-out, scientifically tested, and (so far as we can tell) almost inevitably effective for most products. This sort of advertising produces simple, workaday, understandable commercials that never show up on an agency new-business reel; and *never ever* will win anybody's Festival statuette. Commercials of this type are, year after year, required by, and produced for, knowledgeable, sophisticated advertisers, as they go about their business of selling products, introducing new brands, changing misconceptions, fighting off competitors — just generally trying to earn their corn.

There's a second form of commercial, the "image" type — exciting, entertaining, finely-crafted, attractive, accessible; and often memorable, although the commercial's selling message is not. These commercials make you feel wonderful; however, all too frequently they don't communicate much in the way of a clearly articulated selling idea.

The preponderance of advertising lies between those polar opposites — and is essentially less effective than it should be. Much of today's advertising is characterized by unclear, imprecise strategic thinking, and an over-reliance on execution; with no clear understanding of who called the meeting and why. Such commercials are as uncertain of their heritage as a bar-sinister entrant at a family reunion.

David Ogilvy was the only advertising practitioner able to stand with one unfillable shoe planted firmly in each camp — although, fundamentally, he was closer to Rosser Reeves than he was to Sam Scali. Ogilvy probably wrote, spoke, and produced more advertising common sense than any other man before or since, with the possible exception of Fairfax Cone. Ogilvy was truly a giant in the time of giants, and his books today bear careful rereading, study, and extrapolation. My one regret is that I never worked directly with him; only observing him, instead, as he bustled about his agency, building campaign after brilliant campaign.

If there's one thing I've learned in the writing and producing of 25,000 broadcast commercials, it is that departing too radically from the basic principles of basic salesmanship is an invitation to trouble. Because advertising is not an exact science but rather an opinionable art form, there is no overwhelming, irrefutable evidence as to what works and what doesn't. We all have to wing it, and can only:

1. Study the basics. Know them cold. You shouldn't even think about aspiring to be Picasso until you've proved you can draw at least as well as Gauguin. Many agency art directors and writers today are insufficiently trained in their crafts. They pick up pretty executional pebbles like magpies — ignorant as birds as to the source, content, or utilization of the idea they attempt to manipulate; and utterly unaware of the ultimate purpose of that manipulation. Which is: To sell goods. To move product. To change minds.

No matter what the others do, don't you, as a Product Manager, lose your way. Stay with the basics of basic salesmanship.

2. Try the conservative first. Consumers, your basic target audience, are highly predictable. They respond to the same stimuli, every time, in exactly the same way. *Be absolutely certain* you know cold the hierarchy of appeals and psychology operative in your sale before you embark on any trips into the unknown. Be sure your fall-back position is always open to you — and always in the direction of *terra cognita*. Being the first kid on your block to readapt an old idea and build share is cool. Being the first Product Manager to use a trendy but ineffectual execution technique based only on the enthusiastic endorsement of your agency is not necessarily cool — especially if it blows your market share.

3. Never forget that what you say is more important, by far, than how you say it. *How* you say it lies in the viewer's response, "I saw a commercial with a beautiful white bird." *What* you say is, "Dove doesn't dry my skin." (The viewer says, "I want to try some of that.")

Next to last, a word about agencies. Crusty old campaigners like me are hit with the constant allegation that we're anti-agency. Nothing could be further removed from truth. Anyone who has grown up in the business realizes how priceless, supportive, and agreeable an association with a good agency can be. Most agencies, most of the time, do a good job.

There are, however, some agencies — fad-hounded and driven creatively by borrowings from other art forms — that don't. Advertising for them is an end in itself, rather than being the handmaiden of sales. They are too lazy to do their homework.

They are not to be protected; and, if there's occasional smoke curling from my editorial collar, it's agencies like those that lit the flame.

Most of the time, however, I like agencies, trust them, support them, and promulgate the truth that we couldn't get along without them. The trick for a Product Manager is to lead his agency surely and capably.

That's what this book is all about. Even though there's nothing here in the way of a breakthrough experience, and though you may know the venerable principles as well as you know how to set up a memo, they are principles that can't be articulated too often. Though it may be only revisitation for you, it'll be worth the trip.

4

CHAPTER I

ADVERTISING: HOW DOES IT WORK? OR DOES IT ?

How can you be absolutely, positively sure your advertising is working? Sitting serenely at your desk, digesting breakfast while waiting for the agency to forward their analysis of the latest copy research, how can you enjoy a warm welling-up of confidence that your commercials and print ads are ringing up multiple sales in the market place? How can you know for certain that supermarket shoppers, confronted by a hundred facings of competitive products, are unhesitatingly choosing your brand from the shelf, eschewing all others?

The answer is simple: You don't know; can't know; and, for the most part, don't expect to know.

Modern advertising has been practiced for only about a century. Clearly, prior to the time N. W. Ayer's son listed his father's name on the first modern advertising agency (in order to give his fledgling organization some heft) there were lobbyists and advocates and "wine boomers" and print ads that read as if they had been written by medical con men. There were even some highly competitive ads way back in Roman times, on the walls at Pompeii; and, for the first time in history (and perhaps the last) the art director didn't recommend shooting the commercial in Italy. He was already there.

However, the specialty subdivision of marketing called advertising — an activity where a business person undertakes to reach a particular and defined target audience of prospective purchasers through a specified mass medium, presenting selling arguments about his product or service in a persuasive and memorable fashion — is only a little over a hundred years old.

One of advertising's earliest users, Philadelphia retailer John Wanamaker, is said to have complained, "I'm absolutely certain 50% of my advertising is waste. The problem is, I don't know which 50% it is." Wanamaker was lucky. At least he felt confident that half his advertising was working as intended!

We still don't know precisely how, when, or why a commercial or a print ad trips a buying response, or changes a prospect's point of view from disinterested inaction to "full speed ahead." We can track television messages going into a particular household on a specially programmed cable. We then track purchases coming out of that household through the use of special credit cards that activate scanners at the supermarket, coding product purchases. But mere inference is the best connection we can impose between the two sets of data, and that's pretty cobwebby.

Exactly what happens in a shopper's mind, in the critical microsecond immediately before her hand reaches out and converts a shelf-scan into a purchase? Watch a supermarket browser, faced with a dozen buying choices. All at once there is a sudden movement of the hand forward, and a particular product is hauled off the shelf and dropped into the shopping cart. What's the trigger? What's the memory mobilizer — the mental process that makes a purchase go or no-go?

We don't know. But the researcher who can read minds in that instant when shopper becomes buyer, and who can ascertain the trigger-mechanism of buying, will make millions.

We can uncover what consumers understand from our advertising and can measure how they feel about it through a dozen different research techniques; but we still don't know what random image or persuasion lodges in a viewer's mind and memory when he catches the twentieth airing of a commercial out of the corner of his eye, and arrives at a buying conclusion.

We don't know what occurs when the fifth leaf-by of a print ad stops the reader in mid page-turn and sends him back for a re-read. We don't know when a World Series commercial will evoke a "Maybe I'll call that automobile dealer tomorrow."

How does advertising work? We frankly have no idea what element of advertising conveys thought or imparts a persuasive message or triggers recall. After 100 years, the answer continues to be, "We just don't know; it's a mystery."

There is a considerable weight of common sense suggesting that advertising is variously effective for different product categories. Advertising could easily provide the total purchase determination for a pack of chewing gum or a candy bar. It probably has a great deal to do with the successful introduction of a new cosmetic, and the creation of consumer determination to give the new brand a try.

Advertising probably has less to do with selling a computer, or business systems. It's reasonable — probably likely — that advertising alone has far less impact on the brand determination of high-ticket items than it does on impulse purchases. At least one successful, astute automobile advertising executive has been quoted as

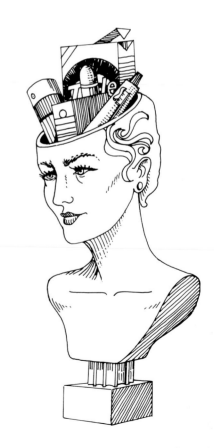

saying, "You can go broke persuading yourself that advertising sells cars."

Sociologists have been largely unpersuaded of the economic value of advertising. Arnold Toynbee, who had a great deal to say on nearly every subject (some of it occasionally relevant), was convinced that advertising is a particularly repellent carbuncle on the body economic.

At the same time, psychologically oriented observers have claimed vast and arcane powers for advertising. They mutter darkly that the ice-cube striations in a glass of whiskey displayed in a print ad will manhandle atavistic receptors in the reader's brain and trip the sex button. (Many of us who work actively in advertising are profoundly grateful this does not appear to be the case. We must, after all, concern ourselves with the continued health and vigor of the GNP, and can't be distracted by such fripperies.) One also expects no mere consumer to dissect an ad with the intensity of the authors of books on subliminal advertising — except perhaps the art director who worked on the ad.

There is reassurance on the basic fact that advertising works and the degree to which it works, in these several sources:

● Advertising is a deductible business expense, according to the Internal Revenue Service. *That* counts. If you deduct it (and the Feds say you can) it's real, all right!

Furthermore, governmental bodies keep trying to tax advertising. That makes it taxable — and therefore even more real.

It doesn't matter that Mr. Wana-maker had difficulty segregating the working 50% of his advertising budget; he got to deduct every dollar.

All the above says there's a substantial governmental body of thought that favors advertising as an effective business method. That should be good enough for you. And for your legal department.

● A much more pragmatic indicator of advertising's effectiveness is the astonishing rise of Procter & Gamble, historically the World's Largest TV Advertiser, from the late 1940s to the mid 1980s. Around the middle of this century, two things happened to P&G: Tide and television.

In the first instance, the product was a runaway success when introduced to a market place dissatisfied with the dingy clothes produced by wartime substitutes. Tide turned in astonishing revenues for the company.

In the case of television, early P&G advertising managers took every bit of their courage and imagination and budgets — all in full supply in Cincinnati during the 1950s — and dumped the works into this burgeoning new medium, which for the first time combined several sensory inputs of product information.

Television married the visualization potential of print with motion, drama, comedy; and added in the color of movies and other visual media. At the same time, it exploited auditory techniques which had proved so effective in radio, and added them

9

to the mix. Best of all, it was an at-house medium. It brought all these wonders to America's living room.

To be sure, during the 1950-80 period, Procter & Gamble also turned out an unparalleled succession of splendid products, launched by an unparalleled succession of brilliant line and staff marketing people. It is often said that P&G's staffers of the day were the most competent any advertiser was ever astute or lucky enough to recruit. None of those people seems disposed to deny that one of the key drivers behind Procter's meteoric ascendancy was the effectiveness of its advertising — television advertising — added to a marketing recipe previously-well-stirred with product, promotion, distribution, sales, and the other factors of a well-rounded consumer marketing plan.

● Direct-response specialists have always known advertising works — and they have precise measurement systems for determining how well it does: Someone simply counts the returned coupons or orders keyed to an ad or to an advertising effort. Direct-response people know right away whether or not they have laid the golden egg or dropped an omelet. Writing for Ogilvy & Mather Direct, David Ogilvy created the slogan, "We sell — or else." Not bad. Al Hampel, former executive creative director of three major agencies, once wrote, "It's not creative unless it sells." That's a good notion, too.

Direct response is where the real advertising action can be seen. Review the basic fundamentals of advertising, and you'll discover many of the principles were first identified and articulated by brilliant, pragmatic, hard-headed, flinty-eyed copywriters who knew exactly what was involved in constructing an ad so the client could sit back and count the responses coming in. If the redemptions weren't numerous enough, the writer didn't eat. How many agency creative people today could make a living under that sort of stricture, with paycheck linked to quantifiable results?

● Another form of direct-response advertising occurs in certain cosmetic and other short-life shelf products that need to generate an enormous amount of initial sale in order to live beyond introduction. A commercial introducing a new hair conditioner or shampoo on Sunday-night network television is expected to clear every single bottle off dealers' shelves by about Thursday afternoon — or the entire effort is a failure.

Again, marketing people in such categories live or die according to the actual, pragmatic, off-the-shelf results produced by advertising.

● One of the most effective practitioners of Advertising-That-Works is the ingenious Francesc Domenech, who runs a young and successful agency in Barcelona, Madrid, TelAviv, and (probably by the time this book is published) a number of other European outposts.

Sr. Domenech possesses one of the most profoundly-developed copy senses I've encountered. He is a superlative creative theoretician; and, for his large Spanish soap client, developed the technique of coming to the U.S. and sitting in a New York hotel room, watching daytime television. His extraordinary sense of what makes advertising effective enabled him to take back to Spain adaptations of the very best of the creative work on American television, which he immediately improved and plugged into his home market. As a result, Domenech's brands in Spain have enjoyed market shares that have historically buried Henkel, Procter & Gamble, Lever Brothers, Colgate — and a whole passel of local competitors.

Domenech knows advertising works — and knows which advertising works. He has proved it time and time again by introducing effectively-selling campaigns in his markets.

From the above, we can conclude the odds are pretty good that advertising works — at least when well used, at least part of the time, at least under certain circumstances, and for certain products. It's a rare agency that would undertake to support the opposing view, although some agency creatives may get a lesser emotional hit out of a share rise than they do from "getting a Bob Giraldi commercial on my reel."

How well does advertising work? How effective is it? A recent study (Effective Television Advertising, by David W. Stewart and David H. Furse, Lexington Books, Lexington, Massachusetts, 1986), indicates that, in a study of 1,000 commercials, there appears to be about a 15% variance in recall, comprehension, or persuasion scores that can be attributed directly to executional factors. In other words, there's probably only about a 15% swing between the worst execution of an idea and the best execution of that

same idea. (And, of course, we still have no reliable relativity established between the idea and sales success.)

Not much meat, considering the

Some creatives get less kick out of market share than "getting a Giraldi commercial on my reel."

cost of the diet! On the other hand, I've yet to meet a Product Manager who wouldn't gratefully accept a 15% share increase — or any percentage thereof, along with the automatic career enhancement that generally follows a share hike. With market points weighing in at millions and millions of dollars-per, any effort that improves the likelihood of advertising's effectiveness is worthwhile.

What is the job of advertising? What exactly is it supposed to do? For Albert Lasker, an early expert, the definition was, "Advertising is salesmanship in print." Another practitioner wrote, "The role of advertising is to help the consumer make a choice" among a range of

I've yet to meet a Product Manager who wouldn't accept a 15% share increase.

products. Leo Burnett used to claim that there is an inherent drama in most products, and it's the advertising agency's job to find it — an early and still cogent case for brand differentiation.

One of the more interesting notions on advertising's function was propounded at least 40 years ago by Mark Wiseman, who worked for

Compton Advertising many years before that splendid agency disappeared into the maze of organization charts known collectively as Saatchi & Saatchi. Wiseman made the startling claim that there's no such thing as selling. At all. In the world. Instead of sales, "There are only 'purchases.' A purchase is defined as *an act of self-help*, in which the purchaser gives up something of value to him (his money) for something *he is convinced will be of greater value* to him — i.e., the product."

Summing up, then:

● We don't know exactly what makes modern advertising sell products — even though we've been messing around with it for centuries.

● We *do* know advertising can have a positive effect on sales, when it has been well constructed and effectively deployed.

● Considering the amount of money involved, we are well advised to take a look at the factors that seem to make advertising work; and to produce commercials which engender Wiseman's "purchases."

CHAPTER II

DO WE KNOW WHAT MAKES ADVERTISING COMMUNICATE ?

After intimate contact with 25,000 commercials, I can't have helped developing some fairly unshakable conclusions, if only implicitly, about which messages communicate and which of them don't.

Over the years, Miner Raymond Associates has consulted for a gratifyingly large number of America's most successful advertisers, each of which seems disposed toward a different method of copy research (ASI, ASI-Plus, Burke, ARS, McCollum-Spielman, Clucas, Phase One, CWI and a dozen other techniques). This huge database of research methods and results led to an interesting observation: Irrespective of methodology, the same factors keep cropping up again and again as having positive effects on both recall and persuasion scores. A cardinal principle as an example: Visualizing a product's end-result benefit in an interesting and

memorable way inevitably leads to enhanced recall and persuasion scores. Yet over half the commercials on today's television fail to Visualize the End Result Benefit (VERB).

To be sure, no one knows precisely what sort of advertising actually moves goods or alters perceptions. But I'd have to have been deaf, blind and distracted not to have noted those factors that enrich recall and persuasion results, irrespective of research method used for testing.

I grew even more interested in the subject when it became utterly conclusive that the research-derived factors boosting recall and persuasion *mirror absolutely* classic principles of selling. Lessons I learned about copy strategy, execution, and communication, growing out of a lifetime of writing, reviewing, and producing commercials, are the same ones that show up in research reports and analyses. What all researchers are reconfirming across the board is exactly what has been the advertising writer's instinctive and empirical creative stock-in-trade for years.

Magazine readers and television viewers in 1989 respond to approximately the same appeals (measured by ARS) as when Burke DAR research measured viewer responses in 1960. Burke's results, in turn, showed up the same as those articulated in CSMI principles (Compton Sales Message Index) in 1953. The same notions as to what interests and motivates consumers surface about every 15 years, regular as clockwork.

These same selling principles were also expressed clearly and vividly in the work of David Ogilvy, who received most of his confirmatory research training through the Starch and Gallup organizations; and they echo Rosser Reeves, whose *Reality in Advertising* was a seminal book of the 1960s (if a much maligned, misunderstood and unread text by subsequent generations). Reeves based most of his inferences and conclusions on solid research results.

Everyone seems to be espousing the same principles. That shouldn't be surprising. If each research method produced a different set of conclusions as to what seems to work and what doesn't, we'd have no concordance of principle. On top of that, if the empirical experience of successful writers and producers were then at variance with all other accumulated knowledge about communication, the advertising world would wobble wildly on its axis, and we'd have marketing anarchy. We've a full supply of that already; we needn't create any more.

One questionably-scientific (but plenty persuasive) technique for convincing yourself that advertising appeals really don't change much

Consumers haven't changed in any of their basic needs.

over the decades, is to go to your corporate library and pull out any magazine published in the 1950s or 1960s.

If you also pull the equivalent publication for a comparable month this year, you'll find the call-outs on the front covers — the come-ons for stories inside which publishers depend on to sell issues off the stands — really haven't changed.

Family Circle still promises "Five Easy Recipes Your Family Will Love." Summertime issues of *Cosmo* and *Redbook* are still promising readers they can "Lose Eight Pounds by Swim Suit Weather"; or that their readers can "Meet and Hold a Man" — even in this age of elevated consciousness.

Consumers haven't changed in any of their basic needs or wants during the hundred years advertising has been functioning in its relatively modern state. Some superficial executional techniques have been updated to reflect contemporary tastes, but advertising's basic hierarchy of needs — security, love, health, a sense of worth, opportunity for self-improvement, hints on leading a full and rewarding life, avoidance of extravagance — all the basic appeals remain essentially the same.

Man has not altered in any fundamental way in 50,000 years, except that today's feed-lot beef has seven times as much saturated fat as that of the wooly mammoth. We still live in condoed "caves," although the mortgage payments are steeper; and, unlike the Victorians (but like the Cro Magnons), both husband and wife work these days in order to meet the modern tax bite.

You can count on the conclusion: People haven't changed much. They love each other, hate each other, fight, fear, love their children, worry about incomes and expenses, and generally struggle to do their best.

Also unchanging in any essential way, are the techniques of communicating through advertising. The first jingle-driven, quick-cut commercial may have attracted some attention to itself simply by being itself; but by now there are jingle-driven, quick-cut commercials on the air for insurance companies and lunch-pail snacks; and automobiles and soft drinks; and beers and chewing gum; and savings and loans and local television stations. The genre has lost its specificity, its distinctiveness and capacity to differentiate — and, therefore, its ability to command attention and send a brand-specific message.

A cogent, dramatic appeal to health, or safety, or comfort — those never change. So, worry — worry a lot and earnestly — if your agency skips over the meat of the sale and starts expounding at length about, and in love with, the execution. Really start to panic if they say, "This commercial will come off only in production. The 'magic moments' are everything." What that unquestionably means is: You don't have much of a strategy or selling idea. You've got a

lot of razzle-dazzle, which is terribly expensive and may not improve research scores one whit or iota.

Another essential communication problem that makes commercials relatively indistinguishable from one another is that copywriters and Product Managers, living for the most part in urban areas, tend to think everybody in America is exactly like they are. Young Urban Professional creative people and account execs convince fledgling Product Managers to make a commercial about *themselves*. Doesn't anyone do store checks any more? Or find out who the consumers really are and what they want?

In my intemperate earlier days, I used to threaten to send every New York or West Coast art director and copywriter to the Ohio State Fair for three days in late August, where they would discover what "sweats" really are. Or to the Hampstead, North Carolina, Spot Festival, where the Volunteer Fire Department sponsors its annual stand-up oyster roast — complete with a precision parachute landing exhibition direct from Camp Lejeune. It's the biggest show in Hampstead, and you meet some wonderful people.

Real consumers live in Columbus, Ohio, and in Hampstead, North Carolina. They work, and strive, and go to church, and bowl, and love their children. They also buy one hell of a lot of beer and cat food and Chevrolets and insurance policies.

If all this is common knowledge, why continue to reinvent patently lumpy or eccentric wheels? We buy trouble in big quantities every time we disregard the basics of selling.

Every writer in America should have

17

been as lucky as I was, some time ago, to be in Salem, Oregon, on the Fourth of July. I was sitting in the local university stadium, waiting for the sky to darken enough for the fireworks to begin. In front of me, resting patiently in the fading light, was a dirt farmer in tattered overalls (nothing "design" about his jeans; you'd have to run them through the lava rock wash for 20 years to match that honorable patina). In his callused hands, nails cracked and split from handling the tools of the earth, was a book of Tennyson's poems. He was reading, as long as the light held.

I frequently think of that farmer when I'm asked to look at yet another commercial involving yuppies at play. I know that my farmer is there in front of his TV set, muting out foolishness and executional fripperies, waiting for an advertiser to say, "Here's how to make your savings safe." When he hears something like that, which really gathers him in, he might even put down his Tennyson.

C H A P T E R   III

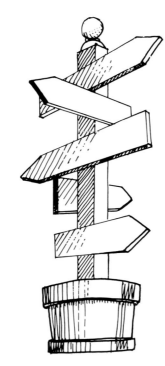

BEFORE
YOU START,
KNOW WHERE
YOU'RE
GOING

A basic failing of much advertising is that clients and agencies start to create it before they know why they are creating it, or what they want to accomplish with it. This may be a failing less of the advertising itself than of its practitioners.

Another fiscal year rolls around. Another brand-new budget is allocated. Another bagful of fresh dollars arrives, begging to be spent.

"Hey gang, let's do some advertising!" or, "Let's put the money in marketing!" carols the group. With no planning beyond that, the conclusion is about as feckless as, "Hey gang, let's put on a show!" The advertising emerging from such aimless effort can be no better than the poverty of its basic planning might indicate.

The underlying structure on which all advertising is built is the copy strategy. It's a well-established ax-

iom; you can bet your share on it: Good commercials grow only from good strategies; and clear commercials are parented by clear strategies; and competitive commercials are rooted in competitive strategies; and wooleymuffle commercials generally derive from like strategies.

The formula proves with any pair of adjectives. The final, absolute, residual, distilled-out message is that *your commercial and your advertising can be no better than the copy strategy on which they are built.*

A strategy is to advertising what a skeleton is to the body. You can be an Arnold Schwarzenegger of execution; but unless you have bones and fulcrums against which beautiful muscles can lever, you're going to lie inert in a large, lumpy pile of motionless (albeit beautifully-sculpted) meat. And so will your commercials. The copy strategy is the structure and framework giving shape and motion and direction and meaning and effect to the execution attached to it.

Writing a copy strategy is one of the most rigorous and demanding activities a Product Manager and his agency can undertake. Because there's such an uncompromising premium on accuracy and specificity in writing ("Overstuffed commercials come from overstuffed strategies, and ambiguous commercials come from ambiguous strategies.") Product Managers and agencies frequently, after a long struggle over strategy, accept the compromise of exhaustion, and settle for something to which everyone can agree — rather than to something everyone knows is right. That concession will eventually come back to haunt them, every time they see the less-than-satisfactory final version of the commercial on the television screen.

Always remember: The copy strategy grows out of the marketing strategy. It is intended to help implement a marketing goal by means of advertising copy. Sometimes, execution problems can be traced right back to an underlying and deficient marketing strategy. It's incredible, but there are actually a few agency executives and creative people in the world who aren't really sure why they are selling the products entrusted to their care. They read the trade press, listen to their bosses and peers. . . and bend with the wind.

Copy failures also occasionally derive from skewed marketing thought placed against a product, with attendant imprecise or unactionable planning. But that's a little rarer.

Generally speaking, if the product is selling at all, many aspects of the strategic marketing thinking are very likely right. It takes an awesomely poor execution to bury a shining strategy. But no amount of executional brilliance can create a marketing strategy that isn't there.

In the majority of cases, however, the most prevalent cause of poor copy is a fouled-up copy strategy, with attendant problems like these:

● **Overwriting**. Some strategies contain every fleeting notion anyone has ever had about the brand. Such strategies are so packed with ideas they couldn't be executed in a half-hour program, let alone a half-minute commercial.

● **Overly "tonal."** We've seen strategies that deal in ineffable terms like, "The product must be approachable, but remote at the same time." Oh, come on! How can an agency creative person seriously accept such drivel as an assignment from a client and hope to turn out an effective execution? (The creative team that got those words in a client strategy couldn't. They went through commercial failure after commercial failure until someone astutely came to the conclusion that it was the copy strategy itself which was at fault.)

● **Inexplicit.** "To convince all women that [brand] is the preferred product." So, what else is new? Give your writer a break: Expressly *what* women? Convince how? *What* should the target audience think as a result of the strategy? Of the advertising? What should they *do*?

An Omnibus Copy-Strategy Format

Here is one version of an all-purpose copy strategy. There is nothing new in the format; it's a compilation and reworking of the copy-strategy elements most frequently used by successful advertisers. Most agencies come up with strategies containing five paragraphs which deal with the following five subjects:

● **Marketing Objective.** *What* are we trying to accomplish through this advertising?

Some may argue that marketing objectives aren't really a necessary part of a working copy strategy. (Those heretics can be forgiven.) A nod in the direction of our marketing goals really should be included right up front, since:

1. The statement of a marketing objective, at the very top of a copy strategy, reminds all of us — those who write the copy, those who submit it, and those who approve it — that advertising is at heart a marketing function, not an art form. Inclusion of a marketing objective serves as a pointed reminder to agency creatives, that winning *Ad Age*'s "Best Commercial" award frequently has little to do with moving cases.

2. The task of boiling down a marketing objective to one or two sentences is an instructive exercise for Product Managers. It validates the agreed-upon marketing conclusion in useful, shorthand form while at the same time teaching those priorities of thought and precision in writing. It also means that, if the Product Manager can boil down the marketing objective understandably to a paragraph or so, it's his; he owns it, as an integral part of him.

3. Placing the marketing objective right up front provides a template against which to measure all subsequent strategy entries. They will have to conform to the marketing goal or they'll look out of place and ring phony.

Defining the marketing objective neatly precludes some obviously misleading conclusions. Take, as an example, the family that goes to Pizza Hut on a Saturday night for supper. They're decidedly not looking for — or buying — the same thing as the family ordering a home delivery pizza from Domino's on Thursday. In both cases, pizza and money are changing hands. But in Pizza Hut's case, the family is buying a fun, casual restaurant experience — a night out. In the Domino's example, the family is buying the convenience of a hot, fresh meal, delivered to their home within 30 minutes.

Clearly, these are not the same products at all, nor will their marketing objectives be remotely similar.

● **Target Audience.**
Who are we trying to reach?

Be as explicit as possible. We frequently see strategy statements that call for a target audience of "women 18-59" and sometimes "*people* 18-

59." Might just as well define your target audience as, "To Whom It May Concern" for all the good it does agency creative teams in visualizing their audience and particularizing their messages accordingly.

Stephen Sondheim, unarguably one of America's most creative theatrical talents and our most prolific songwriter, spoke to the point I'm trying to make by writing this:

"If you told me to write a love song tonight, I'd have a lot of trouble. But if you told me to write a love song about a girl with a red dress who goes into a bar and is on her fifth martini and is falling off her chair, that's a lot easier and it makes me free to say anything I want." *

That's one of the best reasons for being clear, insightful and explicit in copy strategies — to help your agency creatives give you exactly what you desire and need.

It's just possible that the client operating on a strategy with so loose a definition of target audience as "people 18-59" may well be kidding himself about the rest of the strategy too — with predictable results.

If ever there was a "woman 18-59" in this country, there certainly isn't today. Captured in this overcapacious corral are teenagers and grandmothers, married and unmarried, heads of households and "domestic engineers," working and non-working, with and without children, who chew gum or don't, or cook three frozen meals a week at home or don't, or drive their kids to school or don't. The target audience definition has infinitely more capacity for precision than a simple age statement possesses.

And what, pray tell, is wrong with women just 17- or 60-plus, that we should exclude them so cavalierly from consideration?

It's important to assess your target audience as explicitly as possible. Every year in this country we run at least two dozen "commuter" commercials. We show well-dressed, newspaper-carrying people on a platform, getting on a train, getting off a train, waiting for a train, just missing one, with Broadway posters showing in the background.

Does anyone in a New York agency have any idea how *outré* and silly that looks in Des Moines or Dover or Dono Ana, where the mode of transportation is based on the Trailways bus, and rural commuters (who also buy the advertised product by the ton) are more likely to be driving their pickups to a 4-H meeting or a gathering of their investment club?

Does any young person in an agency anywhere have any notion how off-putting or downright irritating yuppies-at-play commercials are to those rich, hard-spending 45-plus-year-olds, whose knees are starting to go but whose pocketbooks are holding up handsomely? It's important to remember Baby Boomers are growing older!

Aside from referring to demographics and psychographics, advertisers often define target audiences on a usage basis, defining "user" and "non-user" targets in terms of frequency of use, tonnage or other highly relevant marketing factors.

The main principle at hand: You look at user and prospect profiles in order to *lay them out explicitly and*

*"The Words and Music of Stephen Sondheim" — *New York Times*, April 1, 1984.

24

understandably for your agency creatives, so as to make it easy for them to see their prospect — to discern who they are supposed to tap on the shoulder. Hammer out as narrow a definition as you can without disenfranchising any singularly important market segment.

● **Principal Benefit.** *What* **do we have to offer the target audience?**

When an advertiser first introduces a product, he knows with considerable precision why he expects people to buy it: He knows from his research exactly which consumer want or need the product fulfills. Presumably, the original marketing reasons still obtain in today's advertising; but *studies show that more than 50% of commercials on the air today fail to visualize the product benefit*. That's shocking! It's also an engraved invitation to a marketing and communications disaster. Imagine a salesman who is so busy being ingratiating he never mentions the rewards and advantages his product will bestow on the prospect.

If this book leads to nothing more than a review of your present commercials in light of the question, "Does this commercial visualize the product's strategic end-result benefit?" it will have been worth every penny of your purchase price.

Today, there are more dual-benefit strategies on the air than ever before — and some of them appear to be working reasonably well. Generally speaking, though, the :30 commercial (and certainly the :15 spot) mean that you are able to convey only a *single* product benefit effectively.

The idea of creating an "omnibus"

pool of commercials — with two or three rotating spots on the air at any given time, conveying and creating ultimate multiple messages — will come up several times over the next ten years, as it has recurrently in the past. Crush without conscience any inclination to consider this idea: It is a snake in the marketing nest. Viewers see but one commercial at a time, and their capacity for remembering a viewing experience across several nights' exposure is not only highly limited, it's nonexistent. Every commercial should be freestanding, entire of itself.

In the broad range of advertising running at any given time, there are precious few dual-benefit strategies. "Great taste/less filling" or "Great taste/low in calories" or "Great taste/convenient," maybe. Not many more that are clearly successful.

You have to be extra wary when promising two antithetical ideas, such as "Extraordinary efficacy at beating grease — yet mildest to hands." Any babysitter who has ever washed dishes knows from her earliest days that this is a canard; that the detergent which cuts dishpan grease so effectively is equally efficient in leaching out all skin oils. You don't gain long-term, loyal customers by attempting to bamboozle them.

The fact that a benefit is not unique or exclusive, but only generic to your product category, is truly not a problem; instead, it enhances the agency's opportunity to shine creatively. "Your teeth aren't white until they Gleem" is a generic toothpaste benefit — particularized nicely to a product. Incisive creative thinking by your agency in a generic product benefit area pro-

duces brand-differentiating copy that makes for high copy-research scores, and increases your chances for high market share.

● **Reason-Why or Support.** *Why can only your product say that and why should I believe you?*

Reason-why makes a generic benefit peculiar to your product and pre-emptive of all other similar products. The woods are full of great differentiating — but utterly generic — reason-why support ideas: Thomas' "Nooks and Crannies," Folger's Mountain-Grown Beans, Hellmann's "Real" Mayonnaise.

Creativity in devising differentiating advertising is where an agency earns its fee. If you've got a generic product, make sure you don't get yourself involved with a generic agency. Instead, choose one that's bright enough to attach "mountain grown" to the beans in Folger's coffee. Clearly, every coffee bean in the world is grown at a certain altitude which could be considered, "mountain." The point is, Folger's appropriated this notion, made it specific and attributable to Folger's, devised a modest animated visual trademark to ram home the idea and make the product distinctive and memorable in the stores. With the help of some nifty marketing, pricing, promotion, and other elements — not to mention the ubiquitous Mrs. Olsen — Folger's went from a small regional roaster to national market leadership in something under 20 years.

● **Brand Character or Image.** *How do we talk, present ourselves to the commercial's viewers?*

This used to be called "tone," but current conventional wisdom is that using the word "tone" focuses agency attention prematurely and inordinately on executional factors, as opposed to strategic or product positioning. If a brand's image is important to maintain (or a corporate image, as is the case with a number of successful advertisers), this is where and how to specify it in the strategy.

But be careful to think it through. Here's a horror story: A network reporter was visiting a commercial set where a creatively-celebrated agency was engaged in shooting a spot for a particular brand of athletic shoes. The TV anchorman asked the agency's creative director — on national television, no less — what he was trying to accomplish. The answer to his question came back something like this:

"Well, you know, like we're sort of trying to talk about a lifestyle here. Like people should be themselves, you know? We're making a statement and looking for, like, a 50s feel, and a lot of neat, unplanned stuff. It's like everybody should be himself, you know what I mean?"

What in the world can we expect the viewer to play back from a commercial executing a strategy as unfocused as this? How would the Product Manager explain it if every verbatim response in the research consisted solely of "Like, you know?" and not one respondent said *anything at all* about these particular sneakers being preferable to the 12 other equivalent, available, generic but differentiated brands?

Clearly, those commercials were not shot to a specific, business-oriented, results-hopeful plan where the advertiser could count on a reasonable return for his investment of commercial-production dollars.

The commercials also lasted a mere eyelid-flick on the air, cost the client a bundle, and the agency considerable prestige. *Sic transit* campaign.

Another Route To Creating A Strategy

Strategic expert Mike Raymond (relationship gratefully acknowledged) defines the process of developing effectual advertising strategies as "one of answering questions." Over the years, the questions don't change; and they can be applied to almost every type of advertising — package goods, automotive, fashion, business-to-business, on down the line.

But even though the questions remain the same, the answers vary radically from category to category, year to year, and marketing situation to marketing situation. It is from the thoughtful, imaginative and utterly relevant answers to these questions that a great strategy can emerge.

According to Mike Raymond, the six questions productive of a strategy that works are:

● What am I really selling?

● Who are the best prospects for what I'm selling?

● Who is my competition?

● What *action* do I want my prospect to take as a result of being exposed to my advertising?

● What do I say to motivate that action?

● How can I get that message to the audience most effectively?

Raymond went on to say, in a speech to the International Franchisers Association, "Of all six questions, the one that is most frequently ignored is, 'What action do I want the customer to take after he or she is exposed to my advertising?' With perhaps the possible exception of corporate advertising, you generally advertise to get customers to *do* something. Don't allow yourself off the hook on this one. Don't settle for an advertising goal that is vague, like, 'Our objective is to increase sales.' And *never* settle for that old chestnut, 'The objective of the advertising is to generate awareness.' You can't take awareness to the bank."

C H A P T E R   IV

THE COPY STRATEGY: WHYS AND WHEREFORES

In the last chapter, I suggested a format to help create solid, directed, competitive, actionable copy strategies. This chapter will outline some of the reasons why you should go to almost any lengths to improve your copy strategy — even though it may represent some of the most frustrating work you'll encounter as a Product Manager. The fervent hope is to get a strategy cleared by management and executed by the agency before the product cycle expires and your brand drifts off to that ultimate Food Giant in the Sky.

Concept: The Copy Strategy Simply Defined

There may be nearly as many definitions of strategy as there are strategies. Here's a definition with the advantage of being simple, as well as workable for a number of package-goods advertisers over the years.

A copy strategy is:

● That portion of a brand's marketing strategy dealing with advertising copy.

● A statement of the basis on which we expect consumers to purchase our product (or retain our message) in preference to competition.

That's it. Let's not complicate the matter. Let's accept the fact that the copy strategy is an intrinsic, essential, integrated part of the brand's marketing program; a message to the agency about the kind of advertising required by, and acceptable to, the advertiser, in order to help bring about a marketing result. An agency ignoring a client's copy strategy — or (heaven forbid) viewing the strategy as an inhibition to artistic expression — is a creative loose cannon. Such an agency assumes advertising is a free-standing art form, rather than an utterly pragmatic exercise intended solely to help bring about positive marketing results.

The second notable attribute of the above definition is that it specifies competitiveness. Strategies written to this definition presume a competitive market. The assumption is that, even if you have developed the first cordless electric shaver outlet capable of working on the moon, you'll have only about six months before someone comes along with a cordless extension that will work on the moon and on Mars to boot. For a few bucks less than yours.

A strategy should have integrated into it, as profoundly and inextricably as genes to chromosomes, the notion of a competitive market situation. The inescapable fact is, we're all operating under competitive conditions.

Now, the fact of competition may or may not imply the existence of a competitive product. If you're marketing a high-ticket item, your competition may be apathy; the potential consumer says, "I'll buy a 20-work-station computer system — but not right now." Or, "I'd like to think about taking a cruise, but calling my travel agent for details is too much trouble." Or, "I might consider buying a new car; on the other hand, I might refurbish my apartment."

This book's simple definition of copy strategy provides for attitude shifts in consumer conceptions about a product. If you're manufacturing an automobile, and the research shows that little old ladies 60 years old and more are the only people buying that car, the competition isn't only all the other automotive entries in your price category; the model's own past image is also competing with you, and possibly inhibiting sales.

Take a look right now at your copy strategies. (First test to be passed: See if you can lay your hands on them.) Consider them against the simple, workable definition here, and the format suggestions in Chapter III. If they don't measure up, note where they fail — and put in a call to your advertising mentor. You're going to need some help.

Purpose: What Does A Copy Strategy Do?

Why should you and your agency work so hard at this uncompromisingly-rigorous writing assignment? A Product Manager has to work hard on a strategy simply because he can't market a product efficiently or consistently without one. As noted before, a strategy is the framework that gives advertising shape and on which the whole marketing effort moves forward. Zero copy comes from zero copy strategies.

A strategy provides these useful and important functions, as well:

● **A copy strategy records and sets down in unarguable fashion all prior agreements on the content and basis of the brand sale.** Like a "bal-

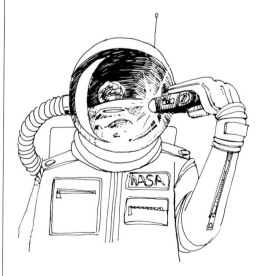

ance sheet for marketing," the strategy describes the brand and its selling attributes as of a certain date and as to be expressed in that particular advertising. A good, solid copy strategy is as important to your brand's success as are reliable financial documents to running a company.

● **A copy strategy provides client and agency with a common reference against which to evaluate advertising submissions.** Think of a typical copy presentation meeting. Into the meeting room, along with the presentation storyboards, come people subject to the common and multiple distractions of any marketing operation. The agency whips out the boards, and everybody starts to look and listen. But, wait! That's the stupidest thing we could do, at this point! The most sensible first step: The agency *whips out the copy strategy and reads it.* If the strategy is well-written, it will take less than 30 seconds to read; and reading it as a preface to the meeting means that everybody in the room starts really looking at the advertising through the same eyes and using the same standards of measurement, thus avoiding potential misunderstanding as well as hours of useless wrangling. Reading the strategy will give all participants a common basis for judging whether or not the advertising performs its primary function — that of executing the strategy.

If, in a presentation meeting, no one refers to the copy strategy, how can anyone tell whether a board is on or off strategy? Nobody remembers every aspect of his strategy so well as to be letter-perfect, without the occasional sneaked peek.

Hence, the first order of business in every copy presentation where significant copy decisions are to be made is the reading of the strategy.

● **A strategy provides a long-term direction and consistency for a brand's advertising.** David Furse, of the Nashville Consulting Group, defines advertising as "a continual dialogue with your target audience." If you switch subjects on an audience you're addressing — rambling off into flights of fancy, changing the topic with every utterance — you'll quickly lose any chance of cogent communication. Your audience will assume an all-too-familiar cocktail-party glaze-over, and will mentally disappear from the immediate vicinity.

The same principle holds true for products and advertising. You may start with, "For the first time in your life feel really clean!" for Zest — and create a whole new strategic notion of exhilaration-in-bathing. Good work! However, if you subsequently introduce the notion of mildness reassurance; then add a few choice words on deodorant protection; next, try to get in some face-washing reminders to ameliorate the bathing message; after that, go down the road of family usage; and finally, try to fight off the beauty bars — by this time, your target audience is confused, bewildered, and well on its way to purchasing another product.

Be assured that almost any amount of time and intellect you devote to creating and maintaining an effective strategy will come back to bless you with share gains and category leadership. You can't ask for more than that from a marketing document.

C H A P T E R V

EXECUTING THE STRATEGY

Now that you and your agency have hammered out a clear, well-defined, actionable copy strategy (and not a moment sooner) it's time to transform the strategy into advertising — to execute your strategy.

What follows is in no way intended to be a checklist of commercial formats, nor does it pretend to be a compendium of advertising execution techniques. There are dozens, if not scores, of ways of carrying out any strategy. This list is offered as a helpful reminder of some of the more frequently-seen commercial types, suggesting that there are many more ways of skinning the strategic cat than resorting to the jingle-driven, quick-cut commercial.

The most often seen commercial techniques include (but are not limited to, as the lawyers say):

● **The aforementioned jingle-driven, quick-cut commercial.** This form is essentially an outgrowth of music video, and occupies a preponderance of the commercial slots on today's television. That's too bad — since research shows such commercials suffer at least a 10% disadvantage in fall-off of breakthrough and persuasion scores simply by employing an execution technique that is essentially *voice-over* (voice heard, as the picture runs its course, as opposed to *direct voice*, which is someone talking directly to the viewer or to someone else on screen).

Also, the quick-cut, jingle-driven commercial frequently lacks continuity or story quality; and that lack will cost still more points. Storyline commercials will generally outscore mosaic or montage commercials with no organizing narrative thread. That's unsurprising; the promises of plot generally invite more viewer attention in search of potential reward, the happy ending.

That's not to say all quick-cut, jingle-driven commercials are inevitably ineffectual for all products and in all situations. It *is* to say that the technique has intrinsic disadvantages, which make it questionable as Scout's Best Bet; and you just plain have to accept those disadvantages as built-in detriments if you choose to go this executional route.

Why in the world, then, would anyone employ an execution technique known to be compromised in its ability to communicate? Frankly, because creative people adore jingle-driven quick cuts; they're relatively mindless to write and simple (although usually wildly expensive) to produce. Buy a $25,000 music track (or contract for an ancient song which no one wants, spending up to $150,000 in the process), and then go shoot 15,000 feet of film — of which you'll ultimately use 45 feet. Even a modestly intelligent chimpanzee could cut together some sort of commercial from that profligacy of picture and sound, given enough time.

You must also face the fact that jingle-driven, quick-cut techniques have completely lost whatever brand-differentiating qualities they might once have had. To prove the thesis, I altered two automotive commercials (Chevrolet's "Heatbeat of America" and Plymouth's "The Pride is Back"), two beer commercials ("The Night Belongs to Michelob" and "This Night Calls for Lowenbrau"), and two soft-drink commercials — switching one soundtrack for the other. Plymouth's track went on Chevrolet's picture, and vice-versa; Michelob's track went with Lowenbrau's picture; likewise, the soft-drink spots.

The results were impressive — and alarming, from the point of view of an advertiser spending real, honest-to-ARS dollars: *Casual viewers in normal viewing conditions didn't discriminate between the commercials!* In fact, since all jingles were written to approximately the same tempo, even the product shots from one spot cut in precisely on the proper sound-track beat of another.

Jingle-driven commercials—deficient in recall *and* persuasion.

It's possible to pull off this sort of switching of track and picture with, say, commercials for an insurance company and a candy bar; or for a retailer and the armed forces. They may match a little less perfectly than the beer or automotive spots. The point is, this experiment is a clear indication that the soundtracks are not explicitly supporting particular, product-oriented pictures. Consequently, there's a disparity between track message and picture message; and that's a violation of Rule Number One in television: The picture and the track *must always* tell the viewer the same thing at the same time, in perfect sync. Fail to observe the rule, and you'll see a measurable degradation of viewer interest and comprehension. You've driven your audience to the mute button.

Never kid yourself that a picture of a man and boy is emotionally loaded

38

with male bonding, while the track talks about insurance. When asked what he saw, the literal-minded, average viewer will respond, "I saw a man and a kid." Nothing about insurance.

● **Testimonial.** This is a much-maligned, grossly-underutilized advertising execution technique — first, because good testimonials are extraordinarily difficult to bring off; and further, because a great many agency people seem to find it easier to castigate the technique than to master it. Creating and producing a believable testimonial is a deceptively simple task, demanding the very best from advertising creatives and strategists.

Think, for a moment, what testimonial advertising has achieved in the way of advertising results. As used by Tylenol, the technique initially created an enormous brand share in the analgesic category, and built unshakable feelings of confidence and trustworthiness among consumers. This consumer confidence withstood enough bad news to have buried 23 other products.

For Folger's Instant Coffee, testimonial commercials took an unpretentious instant coffee and imbued it with so much respectability that it gained important market share; testimonial commercials convinced consumers that Folger's Instant was "Rich enough to be served in America's finest restaurants." P&G made further capital of this notion in a brilliant subsequent adaptation, "Rich enough to be served in your home."

For Jif Peanut Butter, the great "Choosy mothers choose Jif" campaigns out of the Grey agency evolved through a sequence of four or five testimonial executions over a dozen years. They helped move Jif from a perennial second place (to Skippy or Peter Pan, depending on where you lived) to a resounding market leadership, nationally.

The great advantages of testimonial advertising are that the technique — at least, when well conceived and carried out as it is by Lintas, Grey, and a few other agencies — is usually centered dead on the product. Almost always, the protagonist's testimony is built on a foundation of product-in-use, end-result benefit, a before-and-after experience with the product versus a competitive product — or some other actual product experience. Product-centered as testimonial commercials are, viewers are unlikely to stray very far from the commercial's basic strategic message.

Testimonial advertising can also make visible certain otherwise "invisible" attributes (like the good taste of foods) through the testimony of the respondent. Young & Rubicam first used the technique for Cheer in the 1950s, when the primitive black-and-white television system was far too insensitive and grainy to show an advantage in end-result whiteness of a Cheer-washed load of laundry versus an ordinary wash. The system couldn't "see" any whiteness difference in two stacks of laundry, but Barbara Laydenheim certainly could. Skillfully led by announcer Dick Stark, she gave impressive testimony as to the better wash — which, of course, turned out to be Cheer's.

Testimonial commercials can produce memorable "magic moments" few writers are imaginative enough to devise. One of the best commercials Plymouth Voyager has ever run was an extraordinary series of testimonial vignettes, which included this deathless line by an attractive young matron: "Mr. Iaccoca, if you were here, I would give you a-big-kiss-and-a-hug for one of the functional vehicles of all time." Very few writers are capable of writing a line that will juxtapose "a-kiss-and-a-hug" with "functional vehicle"; and few actresses could deliver the line convincingly.

In another magic moment, a director put the package upside-down in the respondent's hand. In response to the inevitable off-screen question, "Want to know what product you've just been using?" she said brightly, "Meegle? Meegle? Oh! [turning the package right side up] *Gleem*!"

This alone had to have been worth a peck of points in recall results.

● **Dramatized problem-solution.** Procter & Gamble used the technique with extraordinary effectiveness during the 1950s and 1960s, calling it "slice of life." That's a misnomer. "Slice of life" is preferably denoted as what it actually is — a problem-solution commercial, set in dramatized form. That description catalogues its great commercial strengths.

People love stories. We will listen to the same story repeated incessantly, and verbatim. Try to switch the Three Bears' beds on your three-year-old, and see how that sells! You'll be firmly and instantly corrected. Life Cereal has brought its "Mikey" commercial back three or four times and can run it to perpetuity (or doomsday, whichever comes first); and we will watch it, slack-jawed and smiling.

From time beyond remembering, the Story-Teller (or priest or legend-gatherer or archivist) has always been the Number Two executive, of the tribe, ranking immediately behind the chief hunter/fighter. Stories — sagas, and legends, and miracle plays, and dramas — are not only an endemic part of every culture; in many cases, they *are* the culture. We seek them happily again and again. Four hundred years later, Shakespeare's plays are still playing to standing-room only audiences all over the world.

As drama, the dramatized problem-solution commercial is validated historically as an effective communications vehicle. It is also an effective advertising device, since generally it is built to encompass a problem-solution format. A protagonist has a problem — because he doesn't use our product. He purchases our product. That gets rid of his problem, and he commences to enjoy a whole batch of end-result benefits, skillfully arrayed and visualized for the viewer's benefit.

It would be hard to devise an execution technique more organically related to the product than this. On top of those benefits, television is a "monkey-see, monkey-do" sort of medium. Watching the conversion of a non-buyer to buyer may well motivate a fair number of the prospective buyers in the audience to emulate the converts on the screen. (It also reconfirms the conviction of buyers who are already steady users of the product.)

Dramatized problem-solution commercials can be — are, in their

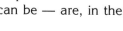

most effective forms — highly competitive. And finally, the utilization of direct voice generally produces a 10%-20% research bonus over any voice-over commercial.

Beware, however, of the agency writer who thinks he can consistently turn out convincing and persuasive dialogue with his left hand. Agency writers who can craft effective dialogue — essential to dramatized problem-solution commercials — are few. The touch required is deft. The opening of a Kellogg's commercial shows how good an ear a writer needs:

Woman: "I can't marry you."

Man: "Why? I'm only six years younger."

Woman: (laughs) "No, I don't care about that."

Man: "What do you care about? My hair? My tie?"

Woman: "Your breakfast."

Man: "This?"

Woman: "Yeah, it's old-fashioned."

Man: "Hey, I'm an old guy."

Woman: "All those years of sugar and preservatives, Bill . . . ."

Man: (groans and fakes fainting)

Woman: (laughs)

Man: "You're right."

No matter how odd it looks on the page, that kind of writing — light, engaging, and unerringly leading to the product and the commercial issue — comes along all too seldom.

By way of contrast, Nissan's short-lived yuppie engineers, lolling around the old design corral, rapping about ergonomics in a language no one ever spoke, failed because their writers failed. The function of a dramatized problem-solution commercial is to tell a story — about the product. Viewer ennui was another reason this campaign was yanked, after a great deal of hopeful exposure, and buckets upon buckets of wasted media and production money.

● **Presenter/celebrity.** Many advertising pundits have said (and I concur) that a celebrity buys you nothing — unless that person happens to be absolutely relevant to the product and to the message at hand. Lynn Redgrave, notable former heavy person now svelte, is as such a most relevant celebrity presenter for Weight Watchers. A glamorous actress is expected not to be a pudgette; and Lynn appears to be agreeably slim — but eminently satisfied by the variation and delicious taste of her Weight Watchers meals and specialties.

Lynn Redgrave is the perfect embodiment (pun absolutely intended) of an end-result benefit. But Charlton Heston for computers? Joe Namath for pantyhose? The mind boggles; reason reels; relevance goes down, fighting feebly.

● **Presenter.** Beyond some extra visibility and credibility, there is nothing a celebrity brings to the party that a non-celebrity presenter can't. Most presenter commercials have the same effect as the forceful personal approach of a door-to-door route salesman. (Don't forget the original definition, "Advertising is salesmanship.") Presenter commercials are usually simple, direct, straightforward presentations of the product and its benefits. It becomes necessary to inject some production value in order to avoid the deadliness of presenter-as-talking-head; but, equally, take care not to overproduce presenter commercials and impair their very effectiveness — which is utter directness and simplicity.

● **Continuing Character.** This is an execution technique which has unnecessarily fallen into recent disuse. But consider how many millions of tons of product were moved by the great pantheon of continuing characters in television — beginning with Charlie, Dash's washer repairman, and continuing with Palmolive's Madge-the-Manicurist, the ubiquitous coffee maven Mrs. Olsen and the early-toilet-trained Mr. Whipple (not to mention Scott's Aunt Bluebell, a particularly repellent member of the species) — *and* Dave Lennox, *and* Mr. Goodwrench. And the non-human varieties: Spuds McKenzie, Morris the Cat, IBM's little tramp. This type of commercial, usually injected into dramatized problem-solution form, is a particularly sturdy variety. If it's currently out of fashion, it is nevertheless long overdue for imminent revival.

There is a problem endemic to the use of a continuing presenters. They have incredible longevity. Josephine the Plumber ran for about 20 years, and Mr. Whipple and Mrs. Olsen were staggering toward their third decade when they finally were allowed to reach decent retirement. That may say something about the technique's acceptability. But it also says you're going to have to beat your continuing presenter to death in order to make way for some different advertising in succession to what has worked well.

● **Demonstration.** Great demonstrations work especially well on television, which seems (occasionally) to have been invented primarily for commercial demonstrations. The antacid's pink-acid beaker turning white; Pampers' endless gallons of blue-dyed liquid soaking into diaper pads; Alka Seltzer's "plink-plunk" effervescing shots; Comet's side-by-side sink scrubs — the literature of TV demonstration is rich and instructive.

Today, when many products are at relative parity in performance, it seems daunting to try to create a distinctive and pre-emptive product demonstration. Do not despair! Instead, do the following:

1. Ask your agency to detail one of their brightest young account executives to the project of finding and testing a television demonstration.

2. Go see your R and D folks — and barricade your scientists in their labs until they come up with three product performance facts capable of visualization. (It doesn't matter that the demonstrations are generic, and common to any product in the field.

As you use them on television — like Rolaids' writing finger — they become yours.)

3. Schedule a day's work at one of the less-expensive production houses headed by a brilliant, visually-minded director in Dallas or Minneapolis. In 1989 dollars, you can buy one of these for approaching $12,000 a day. (However, the sales dollars produced by a good television demo are astronomical!)

4. Shoot a hatful of demonstrations — and pick one to use forever.

● **Animation.** Long disdained by mainstream advertising as being suitable only for Saturday-morning commercials, this category is enjoying a renaissance due to the success of stop-motion, Claymation commercials (essentially a subset of animation) and the antics of Roger Rabbit.

Animation is a great TV technique for the simplest of all reasons: Animation is not "real." In no way does animation pretend or attempt to create verisimilitude or actuality. It is instead visual and aural hyperbole. Tony the Tiger thinks Frosted Flakes taste not simply great — but "GR-R-R-R-eat!" In like fashion, when an animated character wants to show speed, his legs disappear in a blur indicative of the kind of speed provided by the product.

An appropriately broad definition of "animation" includes any kind of frame-by-frame technique:

● Character animation, such as Tony the Tiger.

● Realistic character animation, such as Rusty Jones.

● Diagrams and visual flip charts.

● Stop motion, Claymation, and all its various ramifications.

● Computer optics and graphics.

Animation can do anything you want it to. All your agency needs is perception enough to know what to ask for; they'll find some boffin in a San Fernando Valley garage who can produce your wildest Star Wars speculations at low cost and with little flap.

Clearly, the list above is far from a compendium of available television execution techniques — but, as noted at the outset, it was never intended to be. Nor are these techniques mutually exclusive: You can have a celebrity commercial which is also dramatized problem-solution; or a jingle commercial that tells a story — like Budweiser's best.

The point is, in carrying out your strategy don't settle on a single technique. Look at several before you decide. Also keep in mind that a properly-derived strategy should be capable of execution in several different ways. Occasionally, it's reasonable to ask your agency to work up several alternatives to see which model you want to drive home.

And never forget: *What you say is more important than how you say it.* A strong concept can be executed almost shabbily, and not be damaged. On the other hand, the handsomest execution of "no idea at all" will still be just that: a brilliant technique signifying . . . nothing!

CHAPTER VI

FACTORS THAT MAKE ADVERTISING MEMORABLE AND PERSUASIVE AND THAT DON'T

In Stewart and Furse's book *Effective Television Advertising — A Study of 1,000 Commercials*, the research technique exposed a collection of commercials to a panel of trained raters, who evaluated each commercial on the presence or absence of a given technique. Each commercial had previously been tested by a major copy-testing service (ARS) with respect to recall, comprehension, and persuasion. The book, a technical report of the research results, is already in its sixth printing, including a Japanese edition.

As in much research, the findings from this particular study are easy to over-quantify and misapply, bending in the direction of the bias of each particular reader. Nevertheless, I was led to the writing of this book by the fact that Stewart and Furse's general research conclusions run absolutely parallel to my lifetime's experience of creating and producing commercials for television.

Several of Furse and Stewart's more important conclusions follow. The authors would be the first to echo the caution that these should not be used as a list of strategic or executional "musts." Instead, consider these principles as life preservers for floundering Product Managers and creative people. Checklists are generally despised by creative folk, but they do have their worthwhile functions as reminders and rummaging areas for new ideas. The principles listed here should be sifted as idea-starters rather than discussion-closers. Used that way, they can be most helpful.

Factors That Appear To Affect Recall and Persuasion Positively

● Without question, the most important element to be injected into your commercials is a **brand-differentiating message**. That fact should not be surprising, considering the cavalier way people watch television (see Chapter VII) and the inordinate clutter existing on the air and in viewer's minds. Anything that makes your advertising message stand out by differentiating your brand from competitors and the general background noise of our daily living will pay off. Differentiation is primarily a strategic concern, but it can be an executional consideration as well. Last time I counted (and I barely scratched the surface) advertisers had found over 27 ways of differentiating brands!

● **New product or new features.** Supporting the historic contention that people watch television in order to learn from the commercials while being entertained by the medium, the presence of "new product or features" had the second-highest positive influence on commercial persuasion of any factor in the Stewart-Furse study.

That fact should not come as a surprise. Every year, many thousands of brand-new items show up in supermarkets. Every magazine on every newsstand is full of "new," "different," or "better" ways of doing things, from having and feeding babies to making chicken soup.

It stands to reason, then, that the announcement of "new and better" in conjunction with a product is going to pique viewer or reader interest.

Yet agencies seem to have lost their touch in writing and producing introductory commercials. Writers and art directors, dismissing out of hand the words "new" and "never before" as hopelessly hackneyed, seek ways of cloaking the basic idea of news in all sorts of executional shrouds — like sugar-coating a pill which tastes intrinsically better than its honeyed jacket. Of the introductory-commercial storyboards crossing my desk annually, only about 30% are truly introductory — the rest are the sort of commercial to be run during the third year of a going campaign. Clearly, these came from agencies that didn't fully appreciate the essential strength of introductory information.

If indeed you have something new to say about your product (and it's probably worth a trip to R and D to see if you can't construct or encourage something new and different), for Heaven's sake, say it — as clearly and distinctly as possible. It will increase your persuasion scores.

● Not unexpectedly, the third most influential factor positively affecting recall and persuasion is **length of time the product is on the screen**. The format in contemporary commercials gives the audience a fleeting glance at the product about Frame Six of the storyboard. There may be a second glance at the package — but only in the microseconds before fade-out.

This isn't enough. Ratios and rules are odious — so I'll give you one: You should have three to four clear, uncompromised product shots — as an *absolute minimum* — per :30 commercial. You ought to have two, and preferably three, such shots in a :15; two in a :10; and at least two seconds worth of unadulterated product shot in a five-second ID.

We're talking product shots unimpaired and unobstructed by actors talking, gesticulating, buildings collapsing, or dogs zooming through the stratosphere. "A product shot" should mean exactly that, a close shot of the product, and plenty of what Furse and Stewart heard from respondents: "Time the actual product is actually on the screen."

● **Demonstration.** We've always known demonstrations add up to effective television — since the days of the epic "Baldheaded Sheep" commercial, sponsored by a hair dressing that contained enough lanolin to grease up an inter-city semi. ("You've never seen a baldheaded sheep. That's because wool contains lots of healing lanolin. . . .") Frankly, I suspect that ancient commercial would work just as well today as it did in the early 1950s.

The MasterLock Company of Milwaukee limits its television advertising to one exposure per year on the Super Bowl. From 1973 to 1989, they scheduled essentially the same :30 commercial — an absolutely brilliant demonstration: A marksman puts a 30-caliber slug through a MasterLock attached to a target — and the lock doesn't open! Repeat: does . . . not . . . open!

The commercial's 1973 cost was somewhere around $20,000. In the early 1980s, MasterLock refreshed the pool by shooting some additional scenes. The total production budget: probably under $35,000. Total media

budget? However many millions it cost to run one :30 on the Super Bowl for 17 years.

Demonstration spots are exquisitely suitable for television, because they represent the most direct and obvious route to showing the product, the product in use, or the end-result benefit of product usage. For Bounty and in her heyday, Rosie the Diner Owner presided over three, four, sometimes even five demonstrations within a :30 format! These included monadic demonstrations, side-by-side — the entire pantheon of techniques. They all worked; and it came to pass that the brand became number one; and everyone was happy.

● **Brand-name reenforcement.** If the discovery outlined above is valid, then its confirming corollary is: The brand name should be on the soundtrack as prevalently as the product is on screen. One of the most intriguing scripts I've seen in a long time was one staged in a fast-food emporium, which opened up a whole new usage for Kraft's Miracle Whip. The dialogue runs:

Customer #1: "Hamburger, ketchup."

Counterman: "Hamburger, ketchup."

Cook: "Hamburger, ketchup."

Customer #2: "Hamburger, ketchup."

Counterman: "Hamburger, ketchup."

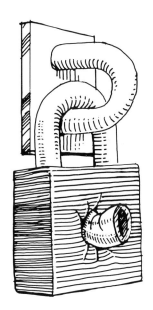

Cook:	"Hamburger, ketchup."
Customer #3:	"Hamburger, Miracle Whip Salad Dressing."
Counterman:	"Hamburger, Mir... Hamburger what?"
Cook:	"Hamburger what?"
Customer #4:	"Hamburger what?"
Customer #5:	"Hamburger what?"
Customer #3:	"Miracle Whip."
Voice-Over:	"Hamburgers, with the tangy zip of Miracle Whip Salad-Dressing. The bread spread makes any thing on bread taste better."
Customer #2:	"Hamburger, Miracle Whip."
Counterman:	"Hamburger, Miracle Whip."
Cook:	"Hamburger, Miracle Whip."
Customer #4:	"Hamburger, Miracle Whip."
Counterman:	"Hamburger, Miracle Whip."
Cook:	"Hamburger, Miracle Whip."
Customer #1:	"Change mine to Miracle Whip."
Counterman:	"Change yours to Miracle Whip."
Cook:	"Change mine to Miracle Whip."

This is brand-name reinforcement exemplified!

Jim Jordan, the multi-talented creative director who has brought forth a hatful of campaigns and splendid execution devices, espoused for some time a technique called "name-monics," in which the name of the product becomes an integral part of the slogan, the claim, the end scene, or some other commercial element. (An example: "Renuzit Doozit.") Namemonics is an interesting technique for brand-name registration and should be explored and exploited. So far as we know, Jordan, McGrath, Case & Taylor has no patent on the notion.

● **Continuity of action.** The alarming proliferation of music-video-type commercials notwithstanding, Stewart and Furse found that presenting a single theme or logical continuity of scenes is a factor importantly and positively affecting recall and persuasion. Continuity means stories; commercials with openings, middles, and closes; with conflicts and resolutions; with climaxes and denouements; ideas developed along a single line — in general, a string of continuous thought along which pearls of information or plot development can be strung in logical, accessible sequence.

Almost without exception, people

are linear in their thought processes. We are taught to think that way from the very beginning, by stories about Dick and Jane. We think — most of us — from left to right and from top to bottom. So it's not surprising that continuity is one of the factors people find acceptable and comforting in commercials — so much so they give it increased attention.

● A close relative of continuity of action has been proved by research conducted over the years by a number of advertisers to be vitally important in positively influencing recall. That is the use of a **continuing commercial character**. This includes all the Whipples, Olsens, Rosies, and Goodwrenches; and may help explain why that genre of commercials is so robust and effective. Talk about continuity of action: Seeing Mrs. Olsen show up time after time with her handy can of Folger's helped burn the brand indelibly in viewer memories.

● **Indirect comparison between products and their unbranded competition.** The Stewart-Furse research confirms what many have always believed — comparison with a disparaged "Brand X" or "leading national brand" or some other inexplicit competitor (no matter how flimsily disguised) can benefit communication. In fact, this sort of comparison is a splendid means of creating brand differentiation — which by itself, as we know, exerts a positive effect on recall scores.

On the other hand, there's at least one exception to the Stewart and Furse research that confirms the rule. A commercial employing indirect comparison was run by a major national package-goods advertiser, and the research results were disappointing. The agency reshot the demonstration sequence, *naming the competitor directly and showing the competitor's package*—and recall scores improved sharply when the commercial was retested.

That, however, is the only case I know of. Conventional wisdom has always held that Americans don't shy away from comparisons. We think competition is nifty; but we tend to draw the line at beating up on anybody in specific fashion. Somehow, that seems like dirty pool, not "the American way."

● **Opening surprise.** The Grey agency used to have a whole Pandora's box full of opening devices to be trotted out whenever recall scores slipped. Feeling the need to beef up a commercial opening, the resolute creatives of Grey would reach for one of their sound effects, such as dogs barking, doors slamming, outrageous lines. ("Bertha, you're a traitor!") The result was always the same: Recall scores jumped.

Common sense says an advertiser has less than five seconds at the beginning of a commercial during which the viewer will reach a decision whether or not he'll devote the next 30 seconds of his life to your cause. Hence, you'd best get on with engaging his interest quickly if you expect the viewer to be there at fade-out.

That means clamp onto his attention and arouse his interest at the very outset. That's also why expounding your principal message in the first five to ten seconds of the commercial is one of the factors which, by itself, positively influences recall and persuasion. Wait until the end of the comercial, and you may have lost the viewer, the sale, the whole game.

● **The general notion of product superiority,** with its attendant technique, puffery, can generate a good bump in persuasion and recall scores. You can almost always find something impressive to say about your product. I've even heard some parity claims in which a poor, homely "unsurpassed-by" notion was trapped out so elegantly it became, Cinderella-like, downright superior. You can also mess around with split claims, such as, "Aspirin doesn't relieve a stuffy nose; Dristan does. Sudafed doesn't reduce fever; Dristan does." — taking on and knocking down your own manufactured straw men, category by category.

Superiority claims or implications are important as a means of helping viewers make choices among various products. This holds true even for parity products which can be resurrected by brand-differentiating creative work, as in an imaginative campaign for Lever's Surf. The argument is, "Some detergents simply mask the odor; Surf gets out the dirt *and* the odor." Getting out odor along with the dirt that traps it is no more nor less than any detergent does. Surf simply picked up an ancient idea, overlooked by Procter, Colgate, and every other detergent manufacturer for many decades, and parleyed it into a highly-respectable market share.

Claims are important. They deserve your very best attention, as well as that of your agency.

● **Humorous presentation.** David Ogilvy once wrote, "The consumer isn't a clown, she's your wife." Of course, he was right. On the other hand, it would be unwise to rule out all humor in advertising. Relevant humor does have a place, as Ogilvy himself conceded. It can sugar-coat an awkward sale or make a dull proposition more memorable.

The problem is to keep the humor relevant to the product and within bounds. This can't be said too often, so I'll say it again: *Keep the humor relevant and within bounds.*

Creative people, unfortunately and frequently, tend to overlook the issue of relevancy. They go for the humor, but forget that it's got to stay related to a sale. When humor runs away with the selling idea, the commercial becomes merely funny, without having meaning for the viewer. Think of all the wonderful, funny Alka Seltzer ads: They sold lots of lines to late-late-show comics, but delivered primarily jokes, catch-lines, and commercial prizes. They were not — repeat, not — effective salesmen.

● **Visual sign-off.** Not surprisingly, the last scene in a commercial is vastly important. It's the picture you leave on the viewer's retina, the last visual impression he or she has before (we hope) confronting your product on the supermarket shelf and deciding to buy it.

There's no telling how many cases of Downy were moved by the simple slow-motion drop-shot developed after I asked P&G Production Supervisor Frank Tuttle to stir up Grey and find something more interesting and meaningful than endless and static shots of bottles on washers.

Visual trademarks or sign-offs are worth their weight in gold. It's probably worth setting your agency on a special creative exploratory in the hope of finding something every bit as good as Visine's "Gets the red out," or Coast's "Eye opener," or Tums' "Tum-ta-tum-tum."

Some other factors from the Stewart-Furse study, positively affecting research results are:

● **Convenience** — ease with which the product can be obtained, prepared, used, disposed of.

● **Sensory information** — taste, fragrance, touch, comfort. Appetite appeal for food products.

● **Commercial setting** — directly related to normal product or use.

Factors That Appear To Influence Recall and Persuasion Negatively

According to the Furse-Stewart study, there are, happily, fewer executional factors that mitigate against a commercial than those which help it — and that's all to the good: We need all the help we can get. Oddly, many of the score-depressing factors cluster around the popular techniques of music videos. For example:

● **Music as a creator of mood** is generally responsible for a fall-off in communication. This is probably due to the fact that, under the guise of "image" advertising, advertisers are led to run commercials which consist solely of mood — and present very

little message for the viewer to remember. Marshall McLuhan was wrong: The medium is only a conveyance of the message, not the message itself: What you say has always been and continues to be more important than how you say it.

● **Use of well-known music.** A previously-popular song contains its own aura of meaning and recollection for listeners; and, no matter how stringently the agency works to imbue an existing tune with a new and particular set of meanings, it will nevertheless continue to retain its former associations. Despite the ardor with which Stove Top Stuffing pushes Stephen Sondheim's "Comedy Tonight" (clumsily retitled, "Stove Top Tonight") people are uneasily aware of a more-than-slight mismatch between the bright, sprightly, patter-song format — and what is a fairly simple and direct message saying, "Why don't you try Stove Top tonight instead of mashed potatoes?"

I've rarely seen the adaptation of an old song brought off successfully. In the course of looking at thousands of commercials, I can't recollect having seen a previously-used song take off and create a sparkling new campaign for a new product. With very few exceptions, the time-honored jingles and musical themes are home-grown and developed from scratch.

Furse and Stewart found that a recognized continuing musical theme clearly identified with the brand is a significant positive factor affecting recall and persuasion, while the adaptation of well-known music tends to have the opposite effect.

Another consideration is that you

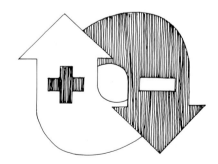

can buy a new tune for far less than you can a previously-owned model — unlike used cars.

● **Graphic displays.** Viewers simply can't see through the graphics thrown at them. People want simple, homely, familiar images; and an artistic head-trip from the latest issue of *Harper's Bizarre* doesn't go down too well in the midst of "Hee Haw."

If your agency wants to use graphics, make sure they're simple and above all relevant.

In the fall and winter of 1988-89, ABC, worried over the persistent decline in the ratings of "Monday Night Football," commissioned an interminable and highly complex graphic opening for the show, involving an analogy between football and a huge pinball machine, with bumpers, thumpers, gates, flying balls, flashing lights, caricatures of Al, Dan, and Frank — a catchall of assorted visual detritus.

It's likely that sports fans might simply have wanted to get on with the football game, find out who was playing, and watch the kickoff — rather than be "entertained" by ABC's minutes of electronic and graphic razzle-dazzle.

The same holds true for commercials; we have all seen commercials where the graphics were so virulent they quite literally destroyed the spots basic message.

● **Substantive supers.** Automobile advertisers are the chief miscreants here. Take any commercial for a special autumn deal — and you can scarcely see the running shots through the thicket of graphics. There are supered titles about the fact that the car in the commercial is driven by professional drivers; interest rates; disclaimers on the interest rates; disclaimers on the areas in which the interest rates can be found. There is also gasoline-mileage information — and disclaimers and hedges on that information to the point where one recent :30 Nissan commercial had a total of 109 words supered on the screen, more than can be uttered clearly in 30 seconds. . . or absorbed by the spot's hoped-for audience.

● **Music as a major element.** One of the off-putting factors leading to low recall and persuasion scores is the use of music as a major element. This is probably very much like the first factor listed — that of "music creating the mood." When scores plummet, music has probably been used as a substitute for the substantive selling message. As a direct result, the commercial fails to communicate anything except at all an agreeable mood. Big smile, nice tone. No message. (No sale.)

Some other factors negatively affecting research results from the Stewart-Furse study are:

● **Information overload** — many different types of information, propositions, or appeals in the same commercial. Lack of focus reduces impact and credibility. Going for too much gets you nothing.

● **Product's physical attributes or ingredients are main focus of commercial** — typically at the expense of demonstrating what the product will do *for the viewer.*

● **Time until product or package is on screen** — needs to be within the first five to seven seconds.

● **Number of on-screen actors**— adds to clutter and confusion; tends to reduce focus on the product.

A repeat warning: It would be wrong to use the principles above solely as a checklist or blueprint for writing commercials. The conclusions disclosed in the Furse research are those which echo what creative people have known all along: People aren't paid to watch television. They are acutely interested in themselves, their families and the immediate state of their afflictions, large and small. They are not avant-garde, they are not disco habitués, and they do like a nice, simple, direct, narrative, commercial with a lot of useful buying information, some news which is interesting and relevant, and a good clear shot of what product it is they're supposed to be buying.

Sounds fairly simple doesn't it?

C H A P T E R VII

Just for the next 30 seconds, picture yourself watching television at home. There's an awesome disparity between the way you, as a professional marketing person, look at commercials during the working day, and the way you as the ultimate and *very* casual audience view them at night, at home.

Production and agency people run commercial footage — and rerun it, and rerun it, and rerun it — again and again on a large screen, flyspecking each square inch of picture, calling on all sorts of optical magic to apply corrections . . . to pictures which should have been correctly shot in the first place. At the prices directors get today, plus heavy preproduction (not to mention those profligacies called prelight days and, "Let's shoot one more for protection.") it's astonishing that any retrospective correction at all is needed.

WHO'S WATCHING OUT THERE? AND HOW? AND WHY?

A soundtrack is recorded — and played back on speakers so huge they could, if unleashed, do permanent damage to the studio walls. Like the pictures, soundtracks are played and replayed, and revised, and sliced, and re-edited, and re-mixed — and perfected to within a dyne of their decibels. Then the commercial goes to the client, and is again put through the microscope, and rerun, and rerun, and rerun — at least three to four reruns for each successive layer in the marketing management hierarchy; so that by the time the final presentation is made, the videotape is close to its maximum-permissible abrasion limits.

In the wholly different environment of the average living room, let's look at the way the commercial we flyspecked so critically during production and approval is viewed by the average American family.

To start with, any commercial is at best an unbidden and unwelcome intruder. People do not turn on their television sets exclusively, or even primarily, to watch commercials.

Any commercial fading up from black displaces program material; hence, it represents a frustration of viewer intent and an open invitation to the audience to suspend attention: converse, scratch, read the paper, push the mute button, leave the room; or attend to any of the several hundred activities that come to mind during an evening's TV viewing.

Aside from the engineer who puts it on the air, *absolutely no one in the free world is being paid to watch any commercial.* Some creative people have even been known to boast about how little television they watch!

The screening of Big-Brother audience tapes — candid views of the TV audience seen from the point of view of the TV set — is instructional and thoroughly humbling. There may be a group of six in the room along with the television set. Of that six, the baby in the playpen is assiduously hammering round pegs into the square holes of his play-school set. Mother and Father are in an argument about family finance, culminating in Father's abrupt departure from the room to get a beer or take a walk, or both. Their teenage daughter is stretching her bubble gum, generating ammunition for her next interminable telephone conversation; while her younger brother is unaccountably studying. Of our initial audience of six, only the family cat is watching the commercial. Unfortunately, the spot happens to be a very good commercial about a brand of dog food.

Every interruption, every off-stage noise, every "Honey, I'm home," every "Mom, he's looking at me," even sudden impinging thoughts and fears tend to thwart the attention and loving care lavished on the commercial by its sponsors.

Exaggerated? Maybe not. Consider for a moment how you yourself watch television. You come home from the office, trailing marketing worries behind you like a snail's track; and on your way past the set, you flick it on. You don't even look at the screen at that point; you attend to the vital and immediate business at hand — securing some liquid sustenance from the kitchen to restore your basal metabolism before mortal flesh flags entirely.

On your way back to the living room, you've picked up the mail from the hall table. Collapsing into your favorite chair, lap full of letters and magazines, you start down through the pile. Your niece in New Orleans remembered your birthday. (The card is two months late.) You also got a notification from the dentist that a next checkup is due; a stiff note from the bank that your mortgage payment is overdue; a letter from your mother (which you saved until last — could be good news, bad news or both). You also have hit the mailing lists for 42 catalogs pushing various products and services, only three of which bear even the most cursory glance.

Meanwhile, the TV set has been pumping out unseen commercials at an awesome rate. To concentrate better on the mail, you hit the mute button — and now, unless you look at the set, all advertising ceases.

The average American does see about 300 commercials daily (Interestingly, and by comparison, the average Italian sees 1,500!) as well as experiencing another 300 exposures to assorted other media — print, outdoor, newspaper, drive-time radio. But so far during this viewing evening, you haven't seen one single commercial—yours or anyone else's.

The mail having exhausted itself as well as you, you take a first look at the TV set, trusty remote-control unit in hand. The first move is shut down *all* networks and *all* independent stations in favor of a previously-recorded sports event you're eager to see. You fast-forward through the commercials which came unordered with your recording, to get to the meat of the football game.

Happy result: Your team won. *An hour* after you turned on the set, you go back to the network, still innocent of any commercial exposure. You take a look at what the networks have to offer, but you "channel graze," switching back and forth to see what's going on elsewhere, every time fade to black signals the onset of another commercial break.

The phone rings, and you answer it. Mute button hit again. You revisit the kitchen to start something to munch on. *Perhaps an hour and 15 minutes after you turned on your set, you see your first commercial.*

Within seconds (according to research), you've probably forgotten it.

Why Do People Forget Commercials?

It's been estimated the average American in the latter half of the 1980s is exposed to around 600 advertising "hits" a day. Of these, roughly seven-eighths of the impressions are forgotten within 24 hours, permanently discarded in the mental "circular file."

This is awesome extravagance, and a titanic waste of sponsor money.

But a small amount of common sense should lead you back to the beginning of this chapter: No one gets paid to watch your commercials. If you want to attract attention to your message, you have to work very hard to earn that attention.

Let's consider, for learning purposes, a few reasons why commercials are consigned to oblivion:

● **Not all commercials are for you.** Commercials can be indexed to attract the specific target audience they are intended to reach. A reference to "sports fans" produces a certain avid, attentive, alert audience, and excuses the balance of the viewing public for the next 30 or 15 seconds. "Mothers" at the head of a track — either verbally or by visual implication — can pre-select such a target audience. The ultimate in indexing I heard in Chicago some years ago, when an announcer hit the airwaves on my car radio and projected, in honeyed tones even Richard Burton couldn't have matched, "Here's a message for hemorrhoid sufferers." After that opening the listener was either painfully attentive, or happily relieved of all listening responsibility for the next 30 seconds.

Indexing can also be negative. The quickest way to drive me to the mute button is to subject me to a heavy-metal track. Whatever roars into my

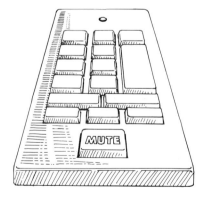

61

living room accompanied by 106 decibels of keening guitar, self-activates my remote-control muting system. An art-director friend says, "I don't allow anyone to scream in my face. And I don't allow TV commercials to do that either."

So, all commercials are not for you; and those that aren't, you'll forget almost immediately.

● **The condition of the viewing mechanism.** The viewing mechanism is you. Immediately before lunch, you will see every food or restaurant sign in your particular part of the city. After lunch, you'll see none of them. Your satiety signal has made them quite irrelevant. Immediately before — and immediately after — buying a new car, you will be the world's most assiduous student of car advertising. Right after your neighbor's garage burns down, you will see every insurance commercial on the air.

At any given time, your condition — financial, emotional, physical — will determine whether or not you are a logical audience for a particular piece of advertising.

● **Distraction and "personal clutter."** As noted above, no one is paid to watch television — and we are all highly distractible by the welter of concerns, questions, and interests that clutter up our lives. The good news, however, is that, despite these many distractions, every single commercial on the air has a 100% chance at its start of engaging attention and folding in viewers for a clear and winning exposition of product benefits. In other words, the engaging and holding power of any single commer-

cial is determined by the intrinsic strategic and creative strength of that commercial. You really don't have to scream in order to get peoples' attention. As Dick Lord, who has worked for or owned several good agencies, says, "You can whisper 'I love you' and get the attention of every hopeful person in the room."

I still see commercials with recall research scores in the high 40s, 50s, and even low 60s. That means the notion of clutter — which has led to all sorts of executional excesses in attempted compensation — has relatively little effect on outstanding selling ideas coupled with effective executions. If clutter applied equally to every commercial, none of them would score above average.

● **Commercials are not as good as they should be.** Despite some high-scoring commercials (and there are, happily, more of these than you might think) average recall and persuasion scores have been flat as a pool table or on the decline for the past several years. I refuse to believe this has anything to do with dulling of the television viewer's taste or surfeit of commercials. Instead, I think that advertisers *aren't learning* from their mistakes, and continue to turn out stuff which simply does not engage or persuade the viewer. At least as measured by copy recall scores, advertising is doing a substandard job in its basic function — which is to provide the audience with a basis on which to make a buying decision.

Average recall and persuasion scores— flat as a pancake.

C H A P T E R   VIII

THE BRAND-DIFFERENTIATING MESSAGE

According to Furse and Stewart, "The single most important advertising executional factor related to the persuasiveness of a commercial is the presence of a brand-differentiating message." The research may be new, but the basic message is not. As early as 1942, one expert concluded that effective advertising "provides a basis for differentiating among products." Giants in the creative process, such as Leo Burnett, Rosser Reeves, and David Ogilvy, promulgated product differentiation through their espousal of "unique selling propositions," "brand images," "positioning," and "inherent drama of the product."

If, indeed, "The purpose of advertising is to help the consumer make an informed choice," then advertising, recognizing and acknowledging its own purpose, must provide the consumer with a basis on which to make that choice.

Over the years, clients who have depended on copy tests as a means of helping appraise their advertising have looked to two factors as measurements of advertising effectiveness — recall and persuasion. These are synergistic characteristics; both are equally important.

Advertising is like a carnival or tent show. If the barker fails to sell enough tickets and there is not a big enough crowd of people in the tent (recall), it really doesn't matter how beguiling are the dancing girls. Your commercial is seen by a too-small audience of people, talking to each other, pursuing agendas of their own — that don't include watching the commercial. Pursuing the carnival simile, the barker can jam a tent with people; but if the show inside is dull, unconvincing, or repugnant, the audience will not stream out after the show onto the midway in the kind of celebratory mood that will lead them to buy cases of Vegetable Revivifying Tonic.

Both recall and persuasion are necessary elements, though research companies, reflecting their individual technologies and heritages, differ on the importance of the one against the other. It is possible that the relative importance of the two measurements may differ according to the kind of product that's being advertised; and, of course, some successful advertisers appear to get along without doing any copy testing at all.

However, the basics of show business — and advertising — are inescapable. It makes sense to get crowds of interested people into your tent, alert for what comes next. Once the show starts, it should be as persuasive as possible, so as to send folks out ready to buy the snake oil.

As mentioned above, there's evidence that recall and persuasion interreact one with the other. Furse and Stewart say, "At higher levels of recall, brand-differentiating messages account for twice the variance accounted for at lower levels of recall." The clear and telling consideration is not, "Which do you believe — recall or persuasion?" but rather, "What can we do to beef up our recall — get ourselves a bagful of people; and once they're inside, persuade the heck out of them?" Meg Blair's research firm, ARS, is presently doing some breakthrough work on persuasion related to media weight that holds high promise for the future.

The brand-differentiating message is your agency's first creative goal. Again, according to *Effective Televi-sion Advertising*, a primary function of marketing communication should be to suggest a basis for consumer choice among products — or between purchase and non-purchase. Advertising is supposed to help the consumer make a choice — to arrive at a *buying decision*.

I have heard it suggested that the primary function of advertising is to inform. Identified are four potential informational areas:

The statement that a brand is superior to competition is a precious asset.

1. Relating a brand to a product function;

2. Implying that a brand is a better buy than other brands;

3. Providing direct information that will help the consumer rank brands;

4. Reminding the consumer of the product, therefore making choice easier.

That may be informational, but it sounds like selling to me.

Continuing this line of thinking, Furse and Stewart have suggested brands can be differentiated in at least three ways:

● **A brand can be *first*.** The first ball-point pen, the first electric razor, the first compact-disc player — "first" products are, owing to the uniqueness attached to primacy, automatically differentiated from all the me-toos that will follow. The sales bonus for being first into the marketplace with a good brand is incalculable.

Rarely do imitative products achieve anything like the market share of the initiator-product.

● **A brand can be** *best*. In the 1980s — the era of emotional and image advertising — claims tended to be downplayed and degraded as being the rational sort of message which doesn't motivate buyers. "Nobody has ever died for a fact." may be an amusing creative argument; but if we support the notion that brand purchases are made on a basis of choice, and that advertising's role is to inform so as to facilitate that choice, then surely the statement that a brand is best or superior in quality to competition is a precious asset.

Far too little time and quality thought is devoted to trying to fly a specific claim through R and D in order to solicit support for it. Creative folk can denigrate claims as "mechanical" and "non-aesthetic." Nevertheless, a legitimate new "Contains no preservatives" statement, particularly when coupled with early entry into the market, can make a brand take off like a rocket.

Claims, representing a reassuring repository of conviction which makes the choice of a brand easier, are important to consumers.

● **A brand can be** *different*. Rosser Reeves' Unique Selling Proposition was, and continues to be, a vitally important method for creating brand differentiation in advertising. According to Reeves, "The role of advertising is to communicate something specific, unique to the product, and important to consumers." What in the name of Ted Bates is wrong with that?

The hierarchy of differentiating techniques that can be applied is endless. Unless yours is totally a me-too product, there is almost no way — given two hours' thought and a trip to R and D — that you can avoid coming up with a statement or positioning which will set your brand apart from its fellows in the marketplace.

Take automotive advertising. For years, automotive commercials consisted of rolling shots through deserts or surf. A current trend outlines the car against cloud effects so heavily backlit and paint-boxed it's impossible to tell whether a Honda or a semi is rolling the road.

Into this welter of cookie-cutter advertising slashed Ford. In 1980, a brilliantly-conceived campaign, designed both to rebuild a tarnished quality image and motivate employees' aspirations to better manufacturing standards, introduced the idea that at Ford, "Quality is Job One." Research findings buttressed the notion (which soon became self-fulfilling prophecy) that Ford was "The Best-Built American Car."

While Ford's other agencies sulked (and although Ford missed the boat in not actively cross-referencing this compelling idea to other Ford and Lincoln-Mercury commercials), the halo glowed over the entire corporation. All of a sudden, Ford — as a company — stood out from the rest of the Detroit crowd.

Furthermore, by claiming quality, Ford effectively preempted every other automobile manufacturer from making similar claims. When Chrysler claimed to be as quality-driven as Ford, people tended to pooh-pooh them *and* their research findings as a severe case of copy-cattery.

How should you differentiate your brand? The answer is simple — any way you can! Here are some obvious areas of opportunity:

● **Strategy**. The formula postulated in Chapter III states, "Brand-differentiating advertising stems from brand-differentiated strategies." If you want to guide your agency toward advertising that stands out from competitors, which staunchly withstands the threat of interchangeability with the advertising of any other brand, you'd better start by building differentiation into the strategy.

A good place to start on a differentiated strategic positioning is with any recent product or market research. Your products or services stand historically for a "certain (specific) something." Over the course of your company's marketing history, there has built up (rightly or wrongly, deliberately or not) a picture of your brand — an image, a positioning, a brand character. That area is an excellent place to start.

Legendary marketing success stories generally follow first-rate differentiating positionings. Johnson & Johnson, through the careful nurturing of its image over the decades, has created a "corporate differentiation" which makes most of its products seem more comfortable, secure, utterly trustworthy than those of the competition.

Procter & Gamble's Pampers has since 1960 stood for absorbency. Cheer originally meant superior whitening; and then, with the advent of colored wardrobes among consumers, switched in brilliant metamorphosis to become the world's first all-temperature detergent, adapting to the mixed wash of the period and newly-available technology of "washing machines that think."

I've heard a thousand protests: "Our agency says we have a parity product, and they can't come up with anything differentiating for us." That excuse may be evidence of a "parity agency"; and you might well think about looking around for a new one. Differentiation — giving consumers help in making a buying choice — is what advertising execution is all about.

For the moment, it's important to say it's *your* job to find a differentiation. Your agency's creative job is to execute those findings with differentiating advertising. You won't find differentiation stuck under the desk blotter; you've got to go out into the field, talk to people, discover what they're thinking.

● **Execution**. In some very few cases, there may be products that are utterly generic and appear to defy differentiation entirely.

Where that's the case, your search is for an advertising idea that can bring differentiation to the product. "When it rains, it [Morton's] pours" has little to do with the molecular structure of Morton Salt. (If ever there was a commodity, salt is it.) However, the statement differentiates Morton *on a performance basis* from any other table salt available to the consumer.

My bet is, despite current advertising, that phrase still rings through the halls of memory when a shopper reaches for the navy-blue package with the umbrella-ed girl on the front.

Brand differentiation is important — so important, it's probably a worthwhile investment of your time to put this book down right now, get a yellow pad, and list the ways to start the differentiation process.

Differentiation will help your advertising. It could help both your sales and share.

What are you waiting for?

CHAPTER IX

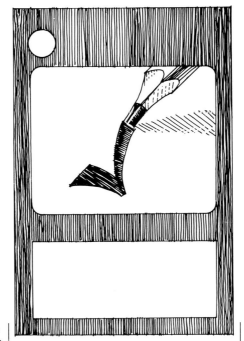

THE STORYBOARD

A clearly-thought-out, properly-detailed storyboard can help head off misunderstandings and avoid booby traps in advertising you're intending to produce, as well as preventing costly executional mistakes, and eventual reshoots.

Some agencies and many creative groups treat storyboards casually, considering them no more than a rough guideline for the finished commercial. Frames may be loosely, even carelessly, sketched — conveying about the same amount of visual information as the stick figures in a first-grader's drawing.

There are usually several reasons for this artful disingenuity:

● The agency does not want to be trapped at rough-cut stage with a well-drawn storyboard which may mismatch the presented commercial in major ways. Such a discrepancy is grossly embarrassing. Keeping storyboard frames loose and indeterminate is playing it safe.

● At the point of storyboard, the agency may not have thought through all the production elements of the commercial — things like camera angles, backgrounds, settings, action; and many of the other considerations that go into the eventual execution of the storyboard. A carefully-drawn and documented board would require those decisions to be made early on, at the time of submission and approval.

(If that sounds like a good idea to you, as buyer of the ultimate commercial, you're right. The storyboard *should* have heavy injections of solid production thinking, up front.)

● Some agencies legitimately expect the commercial director to make a major contribution to the commercial during bidding and pre-production, and they feel keeping the storyboards loose will afford maximum opportunity for that contribution. (I've never seen even a tight, well-planned board discourage a truly creative director from making a deeply-felt suggestion — but that's another story.)

It's an interesting side-note that on-set improvisation is *not* the working method of most legitimate motion picture or television program directors. In fact, a feature director would be thrown off the set if he ever showed up as poorly prepared as some commercial directors. Here's a description of the working methods of one successful movie director: "Most of the director's work — his rehearsals with actors, his planning sessions with the producers, his discussions with the production designer, the cameraman, the art director, the set decorator, the costumer — have been done long before he walked on the set." It's a reasonable expectation that your commercial director adhere to this high standard.

"Magic moments"—unplanned dialogue or pieces of business — do occasionally happen. It's best not to count on them, but rather to plan the basics of the commercial on a well-thought-out, compendiously-drawn storyboard. If magic moments happen, so much the better.

Storyboard Deficiencies and What To Do About Them

Irrespective of its universal acceptability, the television storyboard is inherently unreliable in conveying many of the vital characteristics of a television commercial. There's no way a storyboard can show:

● **Relationship within time.** It's difficult for experts — much less people who haven't seen hundreds of storyboards — to predict just how many seconds each separate idea will take for full development in the commercial itself.

● **Action or pacing.** The speed or rate at which visual ideas are introduced and developed is difficult to convey in a board. The commercial may require a mood-invoking languor, or a faster, Keystone-Kops-chase tempo. Both of these are equally hard to perceive and evaluate at storyboard stage.

● **Color or visual texture.** Storyboards cannot capture or convey the essential qualities of particular styles of photography, such as fashion, appetite appeal; beauty or ruggedness; softness or hardness.

● **The world of sound.** Music, announcer copy and natural sounds — real or exaggerated — will ultimately enhance visualization on the screen. But storyboards lack the ability to convey any of this kind of invisible character.

● Most importantly, **the visual content of the scene itself.** Exactly what should the viewer see, think, respond to in each scene? What should the commercial *show*? That's sometimes difficult to render in a board, although the attempt should always be made.

What can you do to improve chances of an excellent storyboard? Some appropriate — and productive — requests of your agency include:

● **Clear, absolutely explicit frames** — and as many as are necessary to tell the story completely. The drawings can be rendered in a fairly simple artistic style, but they should be carefully planned and detailed enough to show the important action, event, or focus in each scene as perceived by the camera, as well as the scene objective. (More about this in the next chapter.) To achieve finished visualization means someone in the agency's production department has to work with the art director preparing the board. Producers should be expert at catching expensive mistakes before they get out of the storyboard and onto the shooting stage — where they start costing real money; catching them up front is a worthwhile effort.

● **Complete and detailed video instructions.** If the "storyboard" consists of pieces of paper with loosely-drawn pictures, and lines of dialogue bereft of video instructions, that's no storyboard. A board must indicate what the camera and actors are doing or, more importantly, what the camera actually sees.

Video instructions should describe the essential visual content of each scene, as well as any net impression each scene is intended to convey to the viewer — for example, "Mom and Dad are watching television. She produces product and shows it to him."

● **Description of setting, actors, and wardrobe.** These should be clearly and fully set forth, either in the board itself or in an attached set of production notes. It is important that everybody involved in the production of the commercial understands exactly what the locale is. Then, how about the actress? Is she "cute," "attractive," "down to earth" or what? How old is she? Is she smartly dressed, or just casually turned-out, wearing around-the-house clothes? Can her wardrobe contribute anything to her character — or to the general tenor of the commercial? What do the sets look like? How are they propped — extensively or lightly? (The answer can have an unsettling effect on the ultimate cost of your commercial.) Generally speaking, the overall mood of a commercial is established by location, actors, setting, and props. Those elements, as listed and described, should be consistent with the mood established as a goal for the advertising itself.

● **Complicated opticals, superimpositions, or special effects.** I have always gone on the theory that, whatever the creatives dream up, some production genius can execute — in his garage, over a weekend. However, some of the extraordinary effects in today's commercials are difficult to perceive on a storyboard.

Your comprehension of proposed effects can be greatly helped by the agency's preparation of some special boards, in which acetate overlays (or other cut-and-paste techniques) show how tricky effects "build" or look to the viewer. Examples of similar techniques in previously-produced commercials can also be shown, as an aid to your better understanding.

Preparing special storyboards also serves as an early-warning system on complexity. If agency creatives cannot describe in words the effect they want — and can't even give an approximation of it through overlays or paste-ups — maybe their understanding is imperfect. Maybe, too, the commercial, as conceived, requires an effect so complex the viewer won't understand it either.

● **Description of music and sound effects.** Music will affect the mood of the commercial in a major way. It's absolutely vital that you understand and agree with that mood, before you start laying out $25,000 or more for a special music track.

If you don't want to fly for the $1,500-$2,000 cost of a music demo track, ask the agency to play you a record demonstrating generally what they have in mind for music tempo, tone, and spirit. The same recording, given to the ultimate music producer, will enhance communication between agency and specialist when it comes time to actually produce the music.

● **Timing.** The agency when questioned may say, "Oh, we read the copy back at the agency, and it fit comfortably within 30 seconds." I can probably read aloud a commercial in half its specified time — but you won't understand what I am saying; and in any case, such an urgent reading provides no opportunity for expression or interpretation by a skilled actor. More often than not, it's an actor's silences that give shape and emphasis to his words.

On the other hand, copy will sometimes appear to be over-written in the board. That could be because the commercial is intended to have an unusual amount of drive and energy, and the packed track will impart a desired urgency. Or, copy can appear to be under-written; the explanation may be that the actors and announcers need extra time for pauses and "dead air," to create emphasis or to react to spoken lines. Also, copy may have been written short in order to allow for music to be "in the clear" — that is, uncovered by an actor or announcer copy.

Shoot The Board

Don't kid around. Don't get creative. Shoot the board. When you get management approval to produce a commercial, you and the agency have a true moral obligation to return to management the storyboard they approved. Under every circumstance, you *shoot the storyboard — first*.

No matter how beguiling the "magic moment" on location, no matter how persuasive the director and creative people as they approach the production of this commercial, you have, behind you at corporate headquarters, an expectation that a certain kind of commercial (the one storyboarded) will be delivered. It is an abrogation of trust to bring back any piece of execution other than the agreed-upon commercial.

There may be on-set attempts to justify overages, thus: "We have to shoot the director's version while the light is good — then we'll go back and finish the boarded version." Absolutely not! The boarded version is what you went on location to shoot — and that's the one to be shot, using authorized dollars, "while the light is still good."

If the director or agency or creative group are sincerely persuaded their version is an improvement over any idea which occurring up to this point, that version can be shot in the hours remaining before production-day's end. Another option the agency may choose is to shoot the director's version on *their* time (and their money).

It is unwise in the extreme to approve any storyboard until you've been firmly convinced it contains enough information — not only the body content *of* your commercial, as it is written, but clear instructions *about* your commercial and the way you want it produced — to convey the commercial idea precisely to those who will execute the board. Revising storyboards is dogsbody's work, and no one really likes it; however, the time and energy expended up front will save endless amounts of repair work — both creative and financial — at preproduction stage.

CHAPTER X

SCENE OBJECTIVES

The medicine of choice for many a sick storyboard is to devote your time and your agency's best thought and attention to writing accurate, understandable scene objectives.

What is a scene objective? It's a statement, describing in detail *the visual message an advertiser intends his viewers to derive from each scene in a commercial.* Like a copy strategy, the purpose of scene objectives is to establish clear communication between advertiser and viewer.

A more explicit and secondary definition is that a scene objective provides a brief verbal statement, typed under each drawn frame of the storyboard, describing in very simple, unambiguous language the visual intention and content of each scene.

If storyboards were perfect documents — predictive representations of the final commercial, as it will appear on the television screen — there would be less need for scene objectives. However, what the camera lens will ultimately see — and, consequently, what the viewer will see in the proscenium arch of his television set — is all-important. Because storyboards are imperfect communicators, they need every bit of help they can get, up front.

Television is essentially a visual medium. According to one authority (the U.S. Navy, which did an enormous amount of basic cognitive research after World War II), 85% of everything a human being has ever learned entered through the eyes. *Homo sapiens* has always been a sight hunter. Children may learn painfully about hot stoves through burnt fingertips; but we learn to recognize the hurtful beast through our eyes, so as to avoid future encounters. We absorb vocabulary and great ideas by learning to read with our eyes. And we receive through our eyes the more abstract impressions of richness, appetite appeal, delightful experiences, love or fun.

Raucous soundtracks to the contrary, that is also how we perceive television commercials. A good commercial still communicates with the sound off (and that, by the way, is an excellent test of its visual content). Turn off the commercial picture, and what's left is simply radio — another communication medium entirely.

The old wisdom is unarguable: If your agency hasn't visualized an idea within your commercial, you haven't communicated it to the viewer. If it isn't on the screen, it doesn't exist.

Scene objectives are most useful in helping agencies and Product Managers clarify the key visualizations they intend to shoot, thereby improving the advertising. Through scene objectives, it's possible to manipulate visual storyboard ideas prior to production (before the important money gets spent), so that you will reap the richest visual harvest from production dollars. Cross-checking scene objectives with goals derived from focus-group results and copy research can't help but show up any weaknesses in the board.

Scene objectives are of incalculable value to the director in planning his work. Today, far too much production emphasis is placed on commercial execution, and directors inevitably get caught up in the Laocoön coils of technique. On the other hand, Product Managers cannot help being interested in having viewers clearly *see* their cars or candy bars; and scene objectives keep everyone on the proper creative track.

If you can't see it on the screen, it doesn't exist.

Finally, scene objectives help reduce errors. There is nothing, absolutely nothing, more depressing than trotting out your latest commercials for a marketing vice-president, who says blankly, "What's that?"

"That's your new commercial," you say happily.

"There's nothing on that screen that looks like anything I approved in the presentation meeting," he snaps. "Where's my commercial? Let me see that storyboard again!"

Scene objectives can make sure that, before anybody packs up to go to Hollywood, everybody is thinking about the planned production along the same lines visually; and the commercial-bought will be the commercial-delivered.

Here follow a couple of examples of scene objectives:

Scene Objective: To show, through the snackers' reaction, how good the candy bar tastes.

Good luck! At this distance, you would be lucky to see these people are breathing, much less that they are eating anything. From so far away, the source of their enjoyment could be candy bars, chewing tobacco, or something more dubious.

A framing more like 2 on the facing page, tells the advertising story, clearly and visually.

Scene Objective: To show, through the snackers' reactions, how good the candy bar tastes.

Another example is frame 3, following on the next page.

Scene Objective: To show her car as he drives up.

Fat chance of even seeing the car, in this framing. The eye moves from woman to the moving distant car (no brand registration possible) to ocean, to woman again. No viewer will have a chance to identify her car until the last scene in the commercial; and that last scene, that five seconds, may represent the *only* chance to help a prospective customer decide to drop by the desired automotive dealer's showroom.

In answer to the dictates of the scene objective, the commercial's director reframes the shot to show the car, as in 4, on the facing page.

Scene Objective: To show her car as he drives up.

This makes it a commercial about cars, not assignations.

Here are some ideas on how scene objectives can help reduce commercial production costs without degrading in any way the quality of the advertising itself.

Storyboard frame 5, on the next page, is the widest shot in a cosmetic commercial. The situation calls for a lovely woman coming home from a date and starting to remove her makeup at her dressing table.

The scene objective is, "**Show the woman's beautiful skin as she removes her makeup.**"

Frame 6, above is the recommended set sketch for that same scene.

To be noted especially are the open window, with a wind machine to blow the chiffon draperies; a Louis XIV antique, acting as a dressing table; period sconces; and a wealth of architectural detail — none of which will ever be seen in the final commercial.

The scene objective said, "Show *skin*." Despite this, the set designer has gone crazy, calling for a high-fashion period set. Clearly there is disparity — if not conflict — which can and must be reconciled before anyone starts building a set.

A recent study of commercial-production costs, conducted by the Association of National Advertisers, disclosed that those production elements showing the most drastic cost hikes over the last few years have been sets and decoration, props, and wardrobe. In the previous example, the woman was slated for a $2,500 gown. (How many cases of product does a dress move?) The purchase of an antique table might have been another $6,000; and set construction was headed for a total of well over $30,000 in all.

According to the scene objective, however, none of those costly elements will ever show in the commercial, except momentarily and peripherally as the woman sweeps into the scene. The table could be a rented reproduction — or even two planks covered by a ruffled duster. If the director and actress are doing their jobs, the eye must inevitably be captured by the woman's beautiful complexion. Most of the lighting falls on her face; the set is relegated to shadow. *Any* amount of money spent on set, wardrobe and propping beyond basic minimum is likely to be wasted.

Another example: The set in frame 7, facing, was constructed, in order to cover the infamous "any eventuality" in shooting a food commercial. The setting was a diner, and the agency authorized the production house to construct 64 feet of walls (both exterior and counter-back) "just to be sure we're covered."

7.

The scene objective should have been (had it existed): **"To show how our product is better than the competition."** The food products in the comparison were on a plate in front of the protagonist; and the extent of the set actually used was about 12 feet behind the protagonist and about eight feet behind the counterman, on the opposite wall.

A total of 64 feet of set built; a total of 20 feet of set actually used. A more thoughtful reading of scene objectives would have eliminated the waste.

I can hear set designers and art directors contesting, "You're talking about conventional, package-goods commercials. We deal in terms of mood and atmosphere, whose expression in commercials is as important as the product message itself."

In answer, take an actual case where the scene objective was, **"To generate excitement by showing the wild horses of the Camargue, stampeding across the horizon "**(8).

8.

The agency in this case had its heart set on six white horses galloping through a particularly remote region of southern France as an image. (The preproduction meeting called for two entire weeks in Paris with high agency attendance.)

A realistic Product Manager, his careful eye on the exchequer, told the agency to shoot instead in Spain, where costs were materially lower. He also said the background did not matter particularly: A horizon line is a horizon line is a horizon line, whether it's located in France, in Spain, or in Patagonia.

Problem: There were no wild white horses immediately available in Spain. The client's suggested solution? Hire any-colored horses and paint them white! Trained horses were located, rented, painted, photographed, restored to their normal color and returned to their owner at a fraction of the cost of running down untrained wild horses in a French swamp and persuading them to parade in front of the camera on cue.

Never forget that television is a closeup medium. Even the biggest TV set is smaller than a picture window, 300 times smaller than a modest movie screen, and a thousand times smaller than the proscenium arch in theaters. *At least 60% of the time* in commercials, the camera is focusing (or should be) on the product, the package, or on the people who use the product and their reactions to it. Unless the product is a Piper Cub, chances are it will be used within the confined space of a kitchen, bathroom, home, or car.

Hence, any scene objective that says, "To show someone using and enjoying the product" automatically also says not much is needed in the way of sets or props to get maximum desired visualization desired.

Some years ago, an agency decided to recreate in a commercial the movie situation from "The Flight of the Phoenix." (I've never understood why *re*creating an already-shot movie costs so much more than the original production.) The situation was a plane grounded — stranded — in a desert. The commercial plot was, **"To show that the passengers and crew would rather strip the plane than leave behind any of the sponsor's product,"** as in frame 9, below.

There were three choices: First, shoot in one of the scrub deserts surrounding Palm Springs. Second, shoot in Arizona, enjoying all the economies that shooting in Arizona can bring to the budget.

The agency chose the third option, and insisted that the commercial be shot in the only "dune" desert in the United States, an inconvenient location near the Mexican border.

As long as the scene objective read "desert," it really didn't matter whether the commercial was shot in dunes or scrub. The point is, viewers should be looking at the plane and its passengers stranded in **a desert**. Considering all the fascinating foreground situation and dramaturgy, the background was at least immaterial, and at most next-to-invisible.

The production cost premium for shooting dune desert instead of scrub desert? About $400,000-$500,000, in today's dollars.

Finally, here's a frame from a recent commercial. Let's say you had to write a scene objective for this. What's the product? Beer? Cars? Deodorants? Life insurance? Long-distance phone services?

93

Kind of puzzling, isn't it. The answer is blue jeans.

Constructing careful scene objectives at the time of storyboard approval will not only sharpen your commercial enormously, but will prevent all kinds of production extravagance too.

Appropriate Scene Objectives

- To show the product.

- To show people enjoying the product.

- To show some attribute of the product.

- To show the brand name clearly.

- To show that the product comes in two sizes.

- To show how to use the product.

- To show the end result of using the product.

- To show the product in relation to its competitor.

- To show the entire family's joy as a result of the product.

These will keep you on track, producing relevant, sensible, cost-*effective* commercials.

CHAPTER XI

ADVERTISING PRESENTATION MEETINGS: WHAT TO LOOK FOR, HOW TO REACT

You know how it goes. The agency tells you they have copy to present, so you notify all concerned and set a date. (It should be observed at the outset that the most rigorous job you'll face in setting up any creative presentation may be securing one of your company's short-supplied conference rooms. Since that may be your toughest task, that's the one you should start on earliest.)

The great day dawns; and while you have a reasonably good idea what the agency is going to present, you've also heard some elliptical hints from the account supervisor. The first clue is his or her assertion, "We'll have a couple of extra treats for you — something you haven't been expecting." (*There's* a giddy promise!) Second, you find the management supervisor, the total account staff and a full-court press of creatives is

making the trip. From all the above, it's possible to deduce the agency is about to execute a sharp left turn not on the original copy itinerary.

At the appointed hour, everybody troops into your hard-won conference room. Anxiety hangs densely in the air. The agency is loaded for bear: There are more great big storyboards stacked face to the wall than you've ever seen before, and the management supervisor is jollying everybody in sight. Given the number and variety of attendees, it's important to recognize the variety of distractions among those present. You, as described before, come into the room having just lost your best marketing rookie and learned your out-of-stock situation has grown to critical proportions. Your boss has been worried all day about restating profit projections; the agency art director is desperate to get a Leslie-Dektor-produced commercial on his sample reel so he can follow up a lead to potential glory at a new agency. Your brand assistant knows he'll have to make the first comment on the presented storyboards — and knows equally, with sweaty-palmed certainty, that he's going to blow it.

Given this compendium of distractions, what do you do? You come up with the most intelligent suggestion likely to be heard that day, which is, "Before we get into this new advertising, somebody please read the strategy to be sure we all begin the project at the same place."

Brilliant! Reading the strategy is as essential to the launching of a creative meeting as review of the will is to the probate process. If you, your management and your agency start a creative session without understanding explicitly where you're supposed to be going, you might just as well not start running at all.

After a period of unpretty fumbling to see who was prescient enough to bring the copy strategy into the meeting, the assistant account executive finally rummages one out of the copy fact book, and you're ready to begin a productive meeting.

If the copy strategy is a good one, it will take no more than 30 seconds to read. (If it takes longer than that to read, return to Chapter III.) There are no more vital 30 seconds to put on the front end of any copy presentation.

Remember, one of the purposes assigned to a copy strategy is "to provide client and agency with a common basis on which to evaluate advertising submissions." That being so, how can everyone in a creative presentation meeting assess advertising with the same eyes and apply consistent judgment unless they are thoroughly conversant with the copy strategy the advertising is supposed to carry out?

Back in the meeting, the agency reads the first board. The odds are lengthy indeed that you and your agency will both view and react to the advertising in precisely the same way. The agency has been living with this particular storyboard for the past month or more, and knows where every comma is buried. The client is, for all practical purposes, looking at the board for the very first time.

Fighting for reaction time like a wounded boxer, you ask the agency to read the storyboard again — which they do. (Can that thing really be a full 30 seconds long? Seems like a :10 — at the most!)

One minute into the meeting, you're asked to articulate some sort of judgment. And it's desirable that you do. Any creative meeting boosts anxiety levels to almost fatal elevations. When a creative puts a storyboard up on a meeting-room rack and starts talking about it, he has, in that same action, put his selfhood on the rack. Don't ask why this should be — it just is: That's the way creative people are.

A speedy but unobtrusive rundown of the following simple checklist will save everybody's life and sanity, not only for the present, but later, on down the road:

> ## "Will someone please read the strategy?"

> ## Time to read the copy strategy— 30 seconds for a good one.

- Is the commercial on strategy?

- Does the commercial look as if it will appeal to your target audience?

- Is the product the "hero" of the commercial?

- Is the selling idea expounded in a persuasive fashion?

- Is the end-result benefit clearly visualized?

- Is the commercial both distinctive and memorable?

Chances are, the answers to all these questions will be at least to some degree, "Yes" — or the agency shouldn't have brought the commercials to the meeting in the first place.

Since the advertising is generally on strategy and worthy of consideration, you proceed to the second most important act in that meeting, which is to reduce anxiety and enable the creative people to hear subsequent comments: You utter the benediction of a General Reaction.

You should say something appropriate and (if possible) positive about the commercial — assuming it passes the checklist above. You don't have to give away the store, or commit yourself irrevocably to a position or course of action which will come back to haunt you later. All that's required is to reduce anxiety, so as to get on with the meeting.

Examples of helpful comments? Try something like, "There's really a lot to like admire in this board, but I'm sure you wouldn't expect a well-thought-out reaction of the basis of such a short or singular exposure"; or, "The board is absolutely on strategy, and generally speaking, it should appeal to our target audience. However, there are some other aspects I want to consider more closely before I commit myself to a reaction you can take home with you." Those will do the trick. The agency needs a signal that the commercial is at least considerable — that it's worth the time and effort of everyone in the meeting. Your agency wants to know, "Are we in the ball park or even in the same league?" If you can give them that, they'll be able to hear and assimilate subsequent comments in an appropriate, positive context.

There will be occasional creative presentation meetings when the advertising is appalling — off-strategy, gimmicky, execution-oriented, designed for the creatives' sample reels rather than your markets, lacking in end-result benefit with only a skeletal mention of the product, or so generic that you could stick any product's name into the spot and disturb nothing.

When a commercial like this looms, it's better to send a signal to the agency right away that you don't think it's a prime candidate. Comments like, "Why don't we set that one aside for a while and come back to it some time later"; or, "I'm really having trouble seeing the strategy expressed in that commercial. Let's defer reaction until we go through the rest of the presentation" should serve notice to all but the most obtuse that the account executives should take the board out into the parking lot and burn it immediately.

Like many organized religions and

most other human enterprises, copy presentation meetings seem to fall naturally into a hierarchical structure. The greenest member of the product group (about 20 minutes out of Wharton) finds 28 pairs of eyes swivelling her way while the Brand Manager (with no small amount of jovial malice) intones, "Charlene is the newest member of our brand team. Perhaps she'd like to give us a fresh point of view." Charlene, gasping for breath and life, tries to find *anything* in the commercial that seems incontestable, and over which she won't lose her hard-won new job. She says, "I thought women's coats buttoned the opposite way from men's coats." That's at least incontestable.

In many copy presentation meetings, the Brand Assistant starts to make comments; followed by the Assistant Product Managers; followed by the Brand Manager; followed by the Associate Advertising Manager; followed by the Advertising Manager. At this point, the agency's management supervisor pulls out his Mont Blanc pen and for the first time starts to take notes. The inescapable implication: No comments, up to that time, are worth committing to paper.

In order to forestall this embarrassingly-structured recitation — but still produce actionable comments for the agency in the same day they visit the client — a lot of companies today use a technique called "huddling."

After enough readings of the board to make sure every client person in the room thoroughly understands the presentation, the strategy, and the relationship between the two, the agency is excused to get a cup of coffee, make phone calls, or in some other way occupy themselves for half an hour. (Please don't do what one California client used to — send the agency out in 115° heat to kick tires in the parking lot.)

Alone, the client group shares reactions and points of view on the advertising (perhaps using the checklist above) and comes up with a single official reaction to the board, buttressed by only a few subsidiary points *in priority order.*

The agency comes back to hear the client point of view on the advertising, and one client person (Why not Charlene? She's earned it.) delivers that reaction to the agency. Since there are no "voices" attached to the comments, the agency has no clue as to which are more important than others. All statements are equally important and equally actionable.

At this point, wise clients either ask the agency to play back their understanding of the client reaction — and/or ask the agency for a call report, confirming the conclusions reached at the meeting. The reason is the same for both — to "hear back" from the agency that they understand the client's position well enough to articulate it. And to own it, as well.

Within the bounds of good manners, you can feel reasonably unfettered in your reactions at presentation meetings. If a board is funny, you're permitted — nay, encouraged — to laugh or smile. If it's boring, you should probably try not to show your ennui. However, if you're confused, the viewer may be also. Be perfectly honest; say you don't get it.

Be sure to give the agency some

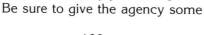

sort of overall reaction, followed by specific comments in priority order. An agency can't extract from a presentation more than three or four comments. If you load them up with a laundry list of 12-15 instructions, each agency person (account executive, creative, art director, producer) will hear only that part of the comment which his agenda allows him to hear; and the discussion on the plane going back to the agency's hometown may be confusing, if not downright acrimonious.

Comments should be limited to basic issues and questions. If you have concerns about the storyboard's handling of one or more matters, articulate them as questions or problems; avoid presenting the agency with solutions. Creative problem-solving is their job, not yours.

Always have a reason to back up your comments — like, "A commuter train station is an unusual setting for this commercial; but will our largely rural target audience, most of whom go to work on the bus, identify with what we're showing them?"

Here are a few don'ts to keep in mind for creative meetings.

Don't make unsubstantiated, emotional, or subjective comments. Stick to the purely advertising issues: Is the spot on strategy or not? Is it "right" for your product or not? Is the product the hero of the commercial or is it incidental?

Don't nit-pick — look at the broad picture and give the agency substantive comments. (You can always forward your smaller comments in writing the next day or so.)

Don't sit on the fence. Everybody recognizes a straddler by the awkward position he inevitably takes.

Don't try to guess the response of others at the meeting; again, toadies are obvious, and odious, to everyone.

Don't give answers — answers are the agency's job. Instead, like Socrates, learn how to ask leading or revealing questions.

Don't insist on winning an argument with the agency at the meeting. If the agency doesn't immediately concur with your point, ask them to "consider it as unresolved" — and then move on.

Occasionally, the agency wants to show you a board which is still stacked against the wall at the end of the regular meeting. They'll turn this one over with some diffidence, saying, "This one really isn't absolutely on strategy, but. . . ."

At that point, stop the proceedings. **Don't** let yourself get suckered into looking at an off-strategy board.

It's happened more than once. The board is indeed a little off strategy — but as winsome as a new baby. If you like it as much as the agency did, you'll probably make an animatic and copy-test it. If it's really great, it'll show up with a high test score. If you get a high score you're honor-bound to produce the board. Probably the viewers will like it as much as you and the agency did. The commercial may very well be effective — and at that point, you will have spent a great deal of money producing highly effective and winning advertising — which, with every exposure, is destroying the strategic positioning you intended for your product.

Don't "pick up the puppy." Say, "I really don't want to waste your time and mine reviewing off-strategy advertising. Since this commercial is off strategy, please take it back and revise it so it is on strategy." You'll save yourself a great deal of time and trouble later on.

Finally, you may learn to be as skilled as one advertising manager who said in a creative meeting, "That commercial is dead on strategy and precisely right in most of its aspects. There's only one thing wrong with it. It isn't good enough for your agency to propose or for us to run. Let's aim higher next time." And he was right. How can any agency complain about a reaction like that?

CHAPTER XII

PRINT —
A PRIMER
FOR
THE
"FORGOTTEN"
MEDIUM

The first cave man who picked up a lump of ochre and went to work on his fire-lit parlor wall was both an artist and our primogenitive print advertiser. Print, as a medium, has been inextricably interwoven with artistic and written methods of communication for as long as there has been publication.

For millennia, print had no real competition. Then, all of a sudden in the middle of the 20th century, two developments came along which brought tough times for print: The first was radio, in the 1920s, 30s, and 40s; the second was television in the 50s, 60s, 70s. Television will maintain preeminence just as long as the networks can continue to get $650,000 for a Super Bowl :30.

Over the past 40 years, while we've been hypnotized by the pretty crystals of the electronic media, print has moved into the shadows both for agencies and at client organizations. Brand budgets are usually built around a certain number of GRPs for network television, with some piecing-out for TV spot, and some very careful media negotiation. For many brands, the few hundred thousand budget dollars left over are devoted to print, almost as an afterthought.

If print has become a relatively second-class medium at client organizations, what happens to it in agencies? New writers, promoted writers, art directors of all sorts have tunnel vision: They see only television. "TV is where it's happening," they say. "The most important thing is to build your sample reel." Print advertising gets pushed lower and lower down the hierarchical structure of glory assignments within agency creative departments.

Consumers and television audiences seem to share these priorities: TV sets gleam and blare into average homes a full 42-plus hours a week. (Whether anyone's watching them, or whether viewers are watching with any attentiveness, is moot.) In contrast, according to the Magazine Advertisers Bureau, American adults spend only about three-plus hours a week reading publications.

However, Phoenix-like, print is rising today from the ashes of its near-demise, and will likely become increasingly popular over the next several years. These reasons:

● Costs of television time and commercial production continue to escalate — without reason, without sense, apparently without control.

● This increase in costs is occurring despite the fact that television viewership is trailing off overall, and fractionating with the advent of cable, VCRs and other means of using the television set.

● The move to shorter-length copy —:15s and :20s — has virtually eliminated television as a medium for a deep, reasoned sale. If you want to present a thoughtful, detailed sales argument with supplementary points and highly particularized information, print's the only place to go.

● On the positive side, the considerable diversification of print media into relatively small demographic segments allows advertisers to reach a much more specialized (and therefore possibly more motivated) audience. The list following is a recent sampling of some of the more popular magazines available in the United States.

Art & Antiques
Town & Country
Southwest Art
Travel & Leisure
Autoweek
Vanity Fair
Car & Driver
Writer's Digest
Car Collector & Car Classics
Yankee
Car Craft
Americana
Circle Track
Architectural Digest
Cycle
Better Homes & Gardens
Dirt Rider
Colonial Homes
Dune Buggies & Hot VWs
Country Living
Family Motor Coaching
Family Handyman
4 Wheels & Off-Road
Flower & Garden
Four Wheeler
Home
Hot Rod
Home Mechanics
Motorcyclist
The Homeowner
Motor Trend
Horticulture
Motorhome
House Beautiful
Rider
House & Garden
Road & Track
Metropolitan Home
3 Wheeling
1001 Home Ideas
Trailer Life

Rodale's Organic Gardening
Boating
Rx Being Well
Chesapeake Bay
Southern Accents
Cruising World
Sunset Magazine
Lakeland Boating
Workbench
Motor Boating & Sailing
The Workbasket
Sail
Esquire
Small Boat Journal
Gentlemen's Quarterly
Trailer Boats
M Magazine
Western Boatman
Penthouse
Yachting
Playboy
American Legion
Modern Romances
American Health
True Confessions
The Atlantic
True Love
Audubon Magazine
Daytime TV
Bon Appetite
TV Game Show
Changing Times
Audio
Connoisseur
Dance Magazine
Consumers Digest
Musician
Ebony
Playbill
Fifty Plus
Stereo Review
Food & Wine
Video Magazine
Games
The American Handgunner

Gourmet
American Hunter
Harper's
American Rifleman
Let's Live
Backpacker
Life
Bass Master
Money
Bicycling
Moneyworth
Ducks Unlimited
Natural History
Field & Stream
Prevention
Fins & Feathers
Psychology Today
Flying
Reader's Digest
Golf Digest
Saturday Evening Post
Golf Magazine
Signature
Gun Dog
Smithsonian
Guns & Ammo
People
Sports Illustrated
Rolling Stone
Time
Black Enterprise
Dun's Business Month
In-Fisherman
Muscle & Fitness
Outdoor Life
Outside Magazine
Runner
Salt Water Sportsman
Runner's World
Sierra
Skiing
Skin Diver
Tennis
Waterski
Popular Photography

Charisma
Christianity Today
Family Computing
Info World
Omni
Personal Computing
Popular Mechanics
Popular Science
Scientific American
Spectrum
Bride's Magazine
Cosmopolitan
Essence
Family Circle
Glamour
Good Housekeeping
Harper's Bazaar
Health
Ladies' Home Journal
Mademoiselle
McCall's
Modern Bride
Ms.
Parent's Magazine
Redbook
Self
Seventeen
Shape
Soap Opera Digest
Teen Magazine
Vogue
Weight Watchers
Working Mother
Business Week
Forbes
Fortune
Inc. Magazine
Income Opportunities
Savvy
Venture
New Yorker
Newsweek
TV Guide
U. S. Magazine
U. S. News & World Report

● Finally, the cost-per-thousand for print is averagely only about 25% of the cost of a night-network :30. This kind of media-cost differentiation cannot be ignored for long.

Differences Between Print and TV Advertising

● It's astonishing but true: Print ads actually compete in an environment of greater clutter than television commercials. Forty percent of magazine pages are given over to ads, while only about 25% of television time is devoted to commercials (perception to the contrary).

● Print requires active involvement of the reader. If the print-ad reader wants to move beyond the page staring back at him, he must stir his thumbs, and flip on. No one will come into the room and turn the page for him. In television, given a single channel of programming, the viewer can watch until rigor mortis sets in, never having to stir a muscle or a neuron. He needs do nothing to move from one image to another; he is spoon-fed predigested fare at a predetermined rate.

● In addition to determining the sequence, the reader also controls the pace of exposure in print, in that he can flip through a magazine quickly, or slowly and selectively.

● Print is a medium for practical information and for directed thought. Buying a magazine at a newsstand — or by subscribing — means an investment of cash or interest in the publication. Television is primarily a medium of free entertainment — with commercials attached.

● It is generally more difficult to write a good print ad than it is to write a good television commercial. Life Cereal's "Mikey" was virtually complete and unimprovable in its first script; David Ogilvy's great Rolls-Royce ads took a lot longer to research and put together; and, in the absence of television's technical and optical wizardry, required a ton more skill in order to catch attention and invite readership.

● Print endures — as any dentist's office will prove. Television ads disappear as they fade to black.

Similarities Between Print and Television

● Just as in television, print must first attract the attention of the casual reader/flipper (which shows up as recall scores).

● Then, the print ad must convince the reader to stay within its borders long enough to allow the sale to work (which shows up as persuasion scores).

● A noticeable print ad has to be at least as inviting and interesting as the editorial material around it — and that makes the agency's creative assignment very tough. It's already been noted that people buy magazines for their editorial content. So if your advertising is going to blow through desirable editorial material to get noticed by the reader, copy and layout have got to be superlative.

● Print can utilize most of the same executional techniques as television — for example:

Problem solution
Testimonial
Presenter
Celebrity
Animation
Demonstration
Slice of Life
Vignettes

● Print ads can be strictly product-related or they can be image-oriented or emotional — the executional techniques are almost as limitless as television's; and a good art director can play with his space, type, and illustration to bring off truly wondrous results.

● While print cannot deliver sound and music, it can provide features TV commercials can't — such as scratch 'n sniff, value coupons, and other promotional blandishments — delivered directly to the viewer's lap.

Do You Have An Effective Print Ad?

Layout in hand, ask the same basic questions you ask about a television storyboard:

● Is the ad on strategy? Does it truly execute an agreed-upon copy strategy? Can you see the strategy in the advertising?

● Does the ad have elements that will obviously appeal to the target audience and deliver them? Will the ad preselect the appropriate readers?

(Again, look at the layout. If you were the target audience, would you stop flipping and start reading?)

● Is the product clearly and visibly the "hero" of the ad? If not — or even "maybe not" — reject the ad and start all over again.

● Does the ad differentiate your brand from all competitors? Could this ad be run for any competing brand by the simple substitution of a logotype? Could it be run for a product or service in another category? (If you've answered "yes" to either of the last two questions — or both — that particular print ad is hopelessly and irredeemably unspecific.)

● Is the end-result benefit shown in the ad? (If not, strongly consider scrapping and starting over.)

● Is the ad at the same time distinctive and memorable?

Components of A Print Ad

While there are substantial variations in format, 98% of print ads have two or more of the following three elements:

A key visual

A headline

Body copy

The Crucial Key Visual

Readers usually look at the pictures first; on average, *65% of the time your reader will spend on your ad is devoted to looking at the key visual.*

That makes the ad's pictorial content absolutely crucial. Don't move on to other considerations until you're satisfied that the key visual is as strong as it can be. At the very least, consider whether or not the key visual should be a page-filling rendition of your product; or your product in use; or the end-result benefit of the consumer's use of that product. Those we know to be money in the bank. You may not be able to improve on them; and it's nice to know you have them as acceptable creative fall-back positions, available at any time.

Don't get so cute that the reader has to resort to mental aerobics to figure out what message your key illustration is trying to get across. Cleverness impresses no one but the author. Always remember, readers aren't being paid to look at your ad. The thumb that flips the page works with awesome facility, and with very little provocation.

You might consider showing your target audience in the illustration. It's also been found that if your model is establishing eye contact with the reader, the ad will attract more attention — unsurprising since we all respond positively to people who are interested enough to look us in the eye, instead of focusing on a spot in midair, somewhere over our heads.

As in TV commercials, key visuals work best when they differentiate your product — that is, they illustrate how your product is better or different from competition. To this end, demonstrations — particularly side-by-side demonstrations — are every bit as effective in print advertising as they are in television commercials.

Key visuals should show either the product in use, or the end benefit, or both; the rule about Visualizing End-Result Benefit (VERB) is probably a more important consideration in print than it is in the electronic media. Nobody ever went broke showing a large picture of why the product is especially good for the reader at hand.

Key visuals should be simple and uncluttered. It's possible to overload an ad to the point where there is no key visual, but rather a collage of conflicting images which rob attention from each other.

Key visuals work best when they are artistically distinctive; however, avoid the temptation of allowing your art director to create a style that exists simply for its own purposes — or for those of his sample book. Seurat may have been a good Sunday painter, by Georges, but pointillism is no way to enhance the presentation of a beautiful lacquered finish on the fender of a BMW.

Don't fall into the trap of mimicking an ad style, simply for its own sake. The technique of a large black-and-white illustration with the logo in color is so "carbon-copy," it's hard to remember who's sponsoring what — if anybody cares, after the ninth variation on the theme. Don't go for fads.

Equally, never fall for the creative chestnut, "This doesn't look like any other [beer] [automobile] [bank] ad." The very good reason beer ads generally tend to look alike is this: That particular kind of execution works.

Headlines

Headlines work hardest when they name the brand. Assuming you've got a great picture of an end result, the product in use, or somebody enjoying the benefits of your product, it does no harm whatever to make sure that the name of the product responsible for all that jollity is clearly delineated in the headline. Naming your product in the headline also makes for unanswerable preemption of your competition.

The headline should, where possible, also state the benefit, as in "Soft Soap for Soft Hands." You're marketing a product for a specific purpose. Why make the reader work hard to discover it? Tell him up front exactly what he can expect.

Be sure to differentiate your brand in the headline. Think of all the ways you can insure the reader remembers that *only* through the use of your brand can he enjoy the benefits expounded in the ad.

Headlines work well in announcing news. As noted earlier, people buy and actively leaf through magazines to pick up new information, new ideas, spiritual refreshment. News is always an interesting topic — especially as set forth in the context of print advertising.

Headlines work hardest when they are provocative — but try to avoid the temptation to approve "cutesie" headlines which are decipherable only after considerable cogitation.

Headlines work best when they offer helpful, product-related information. You should also look for a headline that makes use of specifics over generalities.

Finally, use your headline to flag down and attract your specific target audience, acting as an adjunct to your illustration.

111

It doesn't really matter whether headlines are short or long. We've seen some great one-worders (like Volkswagen's "Lemon"). Equally, David Ogilvy's headline, "At 65 miles per hour, the loudest noise in this car is the electric clock." introduced one of the most memorable print ads of all time. (Maybe one of the lessons there is that a customer thinking of putting out six figures for a car is willing to take more time to read!)

Questions do not generally increase attention devoted to the headline — unless they create a problem to which the advertised product is the only logical solution.

Overall, effective headlines tend to increase recall by getting more people into the tent. Similarly, ineffective headlines tend to work against high recall scores.

Body Copy

Here's a hard fact: The average readership of body copy in magazine ads is only about five percent. Among people seeing your ad, only about 20% will even glance at the body copy. Readership depends on how well the artful use of subheads, running heads, drop initials, ingratiating layout draws that reader into the ad.

Because so little attention is paid to body copy, people tend to think it's of relatively little value. In fact, there arise repetitive creative fads of running "copyless" ads — perfectly acceptable, as long as the total sale is made effectively by means of the picture and headline. Unfortunately, that's not always the case.

The truth is, body copy can add materially to your sale. So why not use it? Long body copy is perfectly okay; if you're interesting enough, people will stay with you, paragraph after paragraph.

Slogans, Coupons, Boxes, Imaginative Logotypes

Yes, to all the above. If they're relevant.

C H A P T E R   XIII

THE HEAVY COST OF RUSH PRODUCTION

Rush, in the context of commercial production, is like a junk-food binge. No one can condone the behavior on any logical basis, but everybody indulges in it more frequently than they wish. There's even a certain amount of self-justification that goes, "Well...just this once." — even as we know, while packing away the enchiladas, that we're going to put on the feedbag many times more than "just this once."

The Association of National Advertisers and AAAA have no trouble agreeing that pressured production is a natural predator of buying efficiency and normative commercial-production costs. However, until now no-one has tried to quantify the cost of rush. There's more than a suspicion that abbreviated schedules cost grievously; but clients are sometimes willing to put up with almost any pre-mium, depending on the urgency of marketing needs.

How much *does* rush cost us? Here are some reference facts and numbers as a basis for better-informed business decisions, when the next time comes to push through a production in record time.

It is axiomatic: A "normal" production schedule for a television commercial is eight weeks from approved copy to air date. Eight weeks is normal; eight weeks, rational . . . and eight weeks, *almost never observed.*

I've shepherded through commercials which were written and approved Friday afternoon, cast Saturday morning, shot Saturday afternoon, edited and approved on Sunday, and put on the air for "Monday Night Football." Two-week production schedules are not unheard of; four-week schedules are, unfortunately, gaining acceptance throughout the industry.

You have not only a right but an obligation to know what departing from the normal eight-week standard production schedule will cost:

● **Bidding.** Shortening schedules beats you up seriously in this department. Worst and first of all, the absolutely-best three directors for the job may not be available on short notice. You may be into a sixth-, tenth-, or twelfth-choice director as the only person free. That creative compromise may be, although incalculable in dollar terms, the greatest cost of all.

On the money side, if you turn up the heat on your agency for rush bids, you can count on the fact that all three bids returned to you will be greased up with 20-40% worth of ugly fat. Panic is highly contagious; and the agency producer who calls the production-house rep in a swivet trips warning sensors that translate into time-and-material padding on nearly every item in the estimate.

The agency may very well tell you, "We have to single-bid this job — we don't have time for competitive bids." This patent nonsense falls in the same category as those other old chestnuts, "We have to have your approval by 5:00 p.m. this afternoon or we'll lose our director." and "The check's in the mail." Clearly, it takes no longer for each of three competitors, working simultaneously, to make his single quote than it takes for *one* person to make *his* single quote. If the agency starts all three bidders at the same time, it will take precisely as long to make three bids as it takes to make just one.

Competitive bidding, all by itself, routinely saves 22% over the cost of single-bid jobs. If you buy the agency's contention that they "don't have time to triple-bid," you're kissing good-bye a chance to save almost a quarter on the production budget, while gaining the aforementioned increment of fat — at least another 20%. Rushing production could be costing you as much as 50% in pads, penalties, and lost opportunities for excellence.

Competitive bidding routinely saves 22%.

● **Pooling.** One of the simplest ways to cut commercial production costs is to gang commercials together in production. MRA-client experience (and I've never seen anybody with better numbers) shows that the second commercial produced along with the first brings the total cost of the pair about 15% below individual costs. Add a third commercial, and you can count on cutting yet another 10%. After that, the economy of scale starts to disappear.

Though you may be moving swiftly on a job, take a look around to see if other commercials can be pooled in with the ones you're planning.

● **Planning.** One of the best ways to get waste out of commercial production is to plan that production with an eye to maximizing efficiency — and, therefore, economy. At the risk of citing Japanese production methods *ad regurgitatum*, Toyota doesn't schedule a red, left-hand front door to show up on the assembly line until *ten minutes* before it's needed. In a rushed-production mode, you'll find yourself overbuying everything you could conceivably need for the shoot (probably about 50% more than you really need, just for safety's sake) on a rush basis at an overtime, crash, insane price. Also lost:

● The advantage a director normally gives you by planning his shots so they dovetail, thereby making the most efficient use of *time* on the commercial shoot;

● The *efficiency* an assistant director creates by planning his people onto and off the set in order to make the most efficient use of their time and your payment dollars;

● The careful planning of post-production to get the work in and out of the laboratories, thus taking advantage of *non-overtime prices*.

When you call for rushed production, you cede back to the production company every efficiency on which you might have gotten a price break. If any discounts exist, the production company will conclude (with an air of pious rectitude, and no small justification) that extraneous dollars should line *their* pockets because of the risk assumed in undertaking the rushed job in the first place.

● **Coverage.** If the agency is exuding panic sweat like a dray horse at a county fair, the director will catch the virus and will triple-cover his shots — just to "make sure" in the screening room. It's realistic to figure your rushed coverage at about 30-60% more than on a normal shoot — with an attendant 30-60% dollar premium added to the cost of personnel time, equipment time, rental, and supplies.

● **Finishing.** Clearly, labs will be working the graveyard shift to get your material out, and editors will be working overtime as well to edit tape as rapidly as the labs produce and transfer it. Those cost premiums can be up to 100% — editorial costs of $8,000-$10,000 on a "normal" :30 will soar at least an additional $8,000-$10,000 over budget.

It's easy to see, then: Rush production adds anywhere from 15-150% to the cost of the same commercial produced on an eight-week commercial-production schedule.

Another handy rule of thumb is that shortening production schedules costs a minimum of 30% extra for each week you lop off. Buy a seven-week schedule, and the advertising costs 130% of normal. A six-week schedule, and you're at a 170% premium. A five-week schedule, and you've probably more than doubled what you planned to spend.

Beyond that, you pay an important — but indeterminate — premium in quality. The ancient wisdom is, "You can have it Tuesday — or you can have it good." Not both.

It hardly bears stating the obvious, that a schedule cut much shorter than four weeks reduces chances of getting a usable commercial to almost nothing. Scratched negative? That scene goes right into the production, scratches and all. Shaky camera move? That's also part of your sales meeting. You may look like a hero, rushing into the meeting with a still-dripping can of film under your arm. But your commercial just won't be as good as it might have been . . . and will have cost an unnecessary multiple of its normal price.

There are psychological costs attached to rush that are harder to assess. What's the morale cost on the agency creative who is always asked to work at forced-draft speed? He cannot do his best work under gruelling deadlines; at some point he plays out and compromises his standards. He can develop no enthusiasm about assignments for inconsiderate clients who push the limits of human endurance. The boy who cried wolf didn't get great copy, he got eaten. The best creatives at the agency may have stipulated with good reason, "I won't work on that account for anything. That client isn't reasonable in his expectations."

What to do about the perennial problems of rush production?

The first step is to recognize and accept the definite, quantifiable costs connected to hurry, and make sure everyone understands them. Some physical and monetary penalties have been detailed already.

The creative compromises you can easily see if you look for them on the screen. The only medicine for rush is preventive: Adopting simple planning procedures makes good sense. A sun-care product manager knows all year long that the selling season is March to early July. In fact, media purchases for the advertising may well be on the books several months ahead of time.

In like fashion, sales meetings aren't called on two weeks' notice. They are scheduled months in advance, as are product launches, dealer meetings, bottler meetings, trade shows, research dates, and all the other events for which clients seem always to have laid on inordinate rush — though deadlines were determined prudently, well ahead of time.

Since everyone knows new commercials are vital for those events, why not schedule deadlines for final copy approval a minimum of eight to ten weeks before? And then schedule copy submissions eight to ten weeks before the approval deadline, so there is time for necessary client reviews or copy testing? That way, optimal advertising is produced on a "normal" schedule — with everyone making a full creative and cost-efficiency contribution, and no one working in a panic and on short rations.

Who can make this happen? *Only the client.* And the only way it will happen is if one of the key client people rears back and says, "I'm tired of spending twice as much as I need to for half-as-good advertising — simply because we can't seem to stick to schedules." When a marketing vice-president memos, "This is important — and I expect agency and brand management to pay particular attention to it." things get done: Schedules are adhered to; deadlines, observed rather than ignored; and commercials are produced on a more reasonable, orderly basis.

The same marketing vice-president should also be told, when he asks for two extra commercials on a

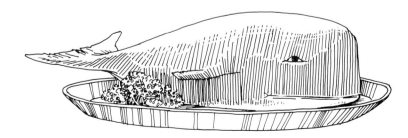

crash basis for the sales meeting, "Okay — but that will cost you an extra $600,000." That's helpful information, which will produce a better-informed business decision. Indeed, it may well be worth the extra $600,000 to have the additional commercials to show at the sales meeting. That's not arguable. Equally incontestable is the dictum that the key decision-maker should always be aware of the costs of rush.

Eliminating rush is like eating a whale: You can't down it all at one sitting, but you can keep taking one bite at a time away in the hope that, over reasonable time, you produce a noticeable dent.

CHAPTER XIV

21
HINTS
ON
REDUCING
WASTE
IN
COMMERCIAL
PRODUCTION

Here's a catechism of suggestions for Product Managers which will enable the reduction of commercial-production costs somewhere between 10-25% — without anyone knowing, from the look of commercials, that anything has been done.

Anyone can make cheap commercials . . . that look cheap. The basic theory (and your primary aim) is to eliminate all wasted dollars in TV commercial production. "Waste" is defined, for the purposes of this effort, as material produced — which the viewer never sees within the picture on his television set. This includes the 60-foot studio set, of which only 20 feet was used (see Chapter X on scene objectives); it also includes the 20 extras that don't even appear within the final frame of the television screen in a crowd scene; it includes the costs of all the time the agency

allowed and you were charged for (but which never got productively used). Conversely it includes all the overtime, crash-schedule penalties you paid simply because there wasn't enough time in the copy-submission schedule to do the job right.

In the interests of eliminating waste, and saving a ton of money, here are some basic pointers:

● **Cut the rush and crisis out of your production operation** (see Chapter XIII, on rush).

Nothing is more wasteful in the advertising process, or more prevalent, than hurry. There are only a few ways to achieve the nirvana of an eight-week production schedule. The most effective is to backtime your copy approval process in order to provide enough weeks for unhurried production — and then force yourself, your management, and your agency to hold to the schedule.

● **Competitively rebid the production, getting three new estimates, where necessary.**

Let's say you get three bids, and they all look just a little pudgy. Your course is clear. Send the agency out for three additional bidders, and tell them to come back within three days with tighter bids.

This is strong medicine, and you don't want to pour it down agency throats very often. However, the technique sends shattering, appropriate signals throughout the production industry; that you're not a "pushover client"; that the original bidders had better shape up and sharp-pencil their estimates; and that new bidders, if they want the work, have an established cost-bogie to beat.

Overall, rebidding is a refreshing, albeit strongarm, measure; but it should reduce costs generally about 22-25%. And you won't be able to see any adverse effects at all in the finished commercial.

● **Insist the agency put an experienced, effectual producer on your business** — the best one in the shop. There is an undersupply of really professional producers in the business; but every agency (except the creative boutiques) probably has at least one. Insist that your agency put the most skilled, knowledgeable, intelligent, independent person on their team, on your account. You'll not only save quantities of money, but will also vastly reduce waste and generally improve the look of your television advertising.

● **Try not to produce commercials singly.** As noted in Chapter XIII, the second commercial in a pool usually reduces overall total costs by about 15%, the third commercial racks up an additional 10% saving. Thereafter, the benefits start to trail off.

If you're a multi-brand advertiser, consider producing in pools of two or more different-brand commercials. I've even seen advertisers, with brands handled by two different agencies, create an "artificial" pool making a two-day shoot out of two single-day shoots; but that's an unusual case, and takes inordinately-secure creative people to agree on a single director, set, and schedule.

● **Cut "versions" out of production plans.** "Let's shoot it both ways." is a clear admission that you are creating a waste situation of at least 50%, since only one version will ever find its way on the air.

It's not easy to pin people down and require them to make tough decisions — but it will, in the long run, save big bundles of cash.

The principal exception to this principle is when you're producing both "new" and "non-new" versions of a product and package — in which case you're well-advised to shoot them at the same time, and save the non-new version for later.

● **Cut linear feet of "wall" out of sets.** In 25,000 commercials, I have never yet seen a set that wasn't overbuilt. Inevitably, sets are oversized, over-propped, over-peopled, over-decorated, and overpriced. The suggestion, therefore, is to call for an automatic and arbitrary 15-25% reduction in set size, with a concomitant reduction in cost. As a bonus, you'll realize commensurate improvement in visualization, from moving the camera in closer to the action or brand. That's usually the important part of the spot anyway. Showing more product, cutting down on "ambiance," means a better commercial.

● **Cut actors out of the story-board.** Your attitude should be, "What's this guy doing in the story-board? Let's get rid of him." Have the agency justify his presence if they feel he's vital. Certainly, before shoot-date the agency should have given you not only a head-count of all people who've been hired (as extras and/or principals — there's a big difference, and be sure you know it) but also a projection of what talent-reuse costs will be. In many cases, the cost of running the spot can be as great as the cost of producing it, and unlooked-for reuse costs (the fees paid actors for re-running the commercial on the air) can put an awesome, unexpected dent in your budget.

Television is a close-up medium. It's better showing a few people than mob scenes, anyway. Mob scenes lose their punch on a 23-inch screen.

● **Cut hours out of shooting days.** The number of shooting hours per :30 commercial has rocketed from six a half-dozen years ago to 16.2, according to a recent estimate by the Association of National Advertisers.

Admittedly, we are shooting more scenes per commercial these days; but there's no need for *almost three times* as much material as a few years ago. The much-maligned (and de-servedly so) quick-cut, jingle-driven commercial is responsible for a good bit of this increase.

One thing is sure: Work will expand to fill the number of hours allotted. Therefore, you should have as a going-in position an automatic reduction of about 25% on the agency's first recommendation of shooting days and hours. Without exception, question the payback potential of all pre-light or rehearsal days; make sure they're clearly justified in dollar terms.

Question all overtime as being probably unnecessary and wasteful. Check the ratio of pre-pro and wrap costs (which don't show on the screen) to shooting costs (which do).

● **Eliminate new shooting by reusing pickup scenes adroitly.** Before you assume all-new footage is necessary, look around and see what you've already got in the trunk. If you've a favorite product pour-shot — or demonstration, or package visual, or beauty shot, or anything else you can reuse — you're manifestly not producing a :30 commercial. You're producing a :22 commercial. The budget should reflect this.

Some advertisers, such as fast-food and automotive clients, shoot libraries of footage for use in subsequent commercials. See if this technique might not work for your product — and cut your budget accordingly.

● **Don't fly New York directors to Hollywood — or vice versa.** Or English or French directors anywhere. Don't take union crews to right-to-

Television is a close-up medium.

125

work states.

Leave people where they are. They know the local scene, and have well-established local sources of supply. Bringing in some big shot from out of town hopelessly complicates the process and ruins the local economy — and ends up costing you a great deal of money.

Remember: Per-diems don't show up on the screen.

● **Ask the agency to investigate good alternatives to producing in New York and Hollywood.** There are lots of other professional production centers — Dallas, Miami, Minneapolis, Toronto, and Arizona. Many southern and western locations are in right-to-work states, which means the requirements to hire exclusively-union labor are superseded by local authority. Take advantage of these markets. If you're going to produce in a right-to-work state, one where union membership is not a prerequisite to employment, don't shoot yourself in the foot by importing a plane-load of union technicians from New York.

Some clients even require that their agencies bid at least one out-of-town production resource routinely on every job. I think it's a fine idea. If your agency doesn't know where to shoot in North Carolina or Oregon, they should find out.

● **Always — Always, ALWAYS! — get competitive bids.** Several fairly reliable and comprehensive studies have proved the mere fact of bidding competitively tends to reduce estimated costs by up to 22%. It's plain foolish not to let the marketplace work competitively in your behalf.

Don't suspend the notion of competitive bidding. It is the single most effective weapon you have against inflated production costs. Get three bids — and inevitably take the lowest one. That keeps everybody involved in the operation honest.

● **Look at commercial-production estimate forms with the same common-sense eye you'd apply to an expense account.** Ask the agency questions; have them explain anything you don't understand. It's your money. Occasionally, ask your agency to take you on a magical mystery tour of every single one of the 300 lines of the AICP form. This will absolutely insure thorough checking before future estimates arrive on your desk.

● **Investigate cost advantages (or disadvantages) of location shooting versus studio shooting.** There are good reasons to consider each — and attendant costs to each, depending on which coast the agency is planning to use. Sets, generally speaking, have a higher price-tag on the west coast; location shooting is generally less efficient in New York. In general, therefore, it makes sense to go west for location and east for studio work. However, it does no harm (assuming there's time in the schedule) to run competing estimates on several different methods of producing the commercial — set or location — in several different production locales. Just remember, no one is at all as interested in saving your money as you are.

West coast for location shoots; east coast for sets.

126

● **Don't worry about making work for the production house by asking them to submit bids.** Remember, the production house that isn't invited to submit bids also isn't getting any work. You're doing production companies a favor by letting them bid on your work in the first place

Don't accept special bidding or accounting charges. If the production house wants to buy a computer so they can bid more efficiently, that's their business.

● **Eliminate out-of-season location shoots.** Plan beach scenes for August and snow and skiing scenes for February. Without that, you're buying an awesome creative displacement — and an even worse production bill. Here again, scheduling is the key. If yours is a suntan product, and you know you're running most of your media April through July, commercials need to be shot the previous fall. Or in Puerto Rico. (No skin product ever looks good going on over goose- pimpled flesh, and it can be chilly all winter in Florida.)

● **Don't be afraid to set a maximum price on commercials.** Establish and discuss commercial costs with the agency as if they were the important subject they are. Discuss waste with the agency as if it were an even more important subject. It is. Set aside a day or two to discuss the whole question of production efficiency. It's a subject very few clients bring up, but one which can save a great deal of money in the long run. The agency has no motivation to save money unless you exhibit more than a polite interest in the subject.

Don't forget most agencies have low-budget clients as well as open-handed ones. They can operate at almost any level of production sophistication. *Make* them be as good as they *can* be.

● **Eliminate all contingencies in bidding.** In the same way work expands to fill the time available, expenditures swell to sop up every dollar in the budget.

Help stamp out this known human failing by eliminating all production contingencies. They're inevitably spent, and hard to trace. Instead, ask the agency to justify overages by securing client approval either in advance, or *immediately* after the overruns have been occasioned. That way, you can learn from overages, and avoid them in the future.

● **Don't buy an overall weather-day contingency.** Tell the agency you'll pay verifiable out-of-pocket, plus 15%. That's it. No more. Weather days — which actually cost the production company somewhere around $9,000-$17,000—are estimated and billed out at up to $65,000!

● **Sharply reduce the number of visitors to the set.** Show business is a lot of fun, and attracts supernumeraries. However, every extra body on the set not only causes confusion, but also uses up time in miniscule or larger proportions — and time is money. I've even seen, on occasion, members of a crew on a shooting set entertaining visitors — just as if *they* were paying for the shoot.

Generally speaking, a commercial shooting-set is no different from any other business enterprise, and the climate should be as business-like and efficient as possible. The fact that production has some trappings of show business encourages a kind of larky atmosphere; but, as a client representative, you will be well-advised to discourage the number of people hanging around. Ban families, friends, associates from the area; and close the set to casual visitors. Meet your friends for drinks afterward. You wouldn't allow people to hang around your office during a workday; there's no reason for condoning such laxity on a commercial stage.

● **Cut repetitive takes out of your shooting schedule.** We've all seen it happen: Everybody agrees that Take Six is "pretty good" — agency, producer, director, and client. Then some idiot says, "But let's get one for insurance," and 46 takes later the director has glazed over with ennui, the actors can't remember where the stresses in the line are supposed to fall, and you've blown about an hour's time to absolutely no worthwhile production consequence.

Use VTR playbacks to check your judgment (*not* to supplant it); and when you've got a good take that everybody likes, mark it and move on to the next one.

The principal questions to be asked on any production enterprise are, "Do we really need this? Will it sell one additional case of product? Will this piece of business even be seen on the screen in the final version?"

If all you do is reduce the waste from your shooting — simply eliminating the stuff that no one's going to see — you'll save 15-25%. Those dollars are certainly worth going after. Good hunting to you!

CHAPTER XV

THE PREPRODUCTION MEETING

The preproduction meeting is a critical moment in a television commercial's life — when the immediate responsibility for the advertising is transferred from those who have conceived the storyboard and nurtured it — all the way from ephemeral idea, through script revisions, copy strengthening, legal clearance, network clearance and 65 layers of agency and client approval — to those who are going to turn those silent words and motionless pictures into an actual, living, breathing, on-air television commercial.

As in many transfer operations, there are endless perils and opportunities for expensive, demoralizing misunderstandings, mishandlings, and just plain mistakes.

Whether or not your cygnet storyboard evolves into a gliding swan among the ducklings of the station-break depends in large measure on how successful your preproduction meeting was. Whether or not you handle production money wisely, and come out with all possibilities covered (yet without waste) also hangs, to a major degree, on the preproduction meeting. Whether or not the commercial is carried by outstanding actors who will be memorable (thereby lending memorability and credibility to your product) depends on success in casting, which has its culmination in talent approval at preproduction.

The best insurance for a good commercial shoot is a thorough preproduction meeting — one in which the overall objectives of the advertising and the specific objectives of each scene are verbalized and confirmed; along with all the other decisions that must be made, including sets and decoration, props, costuming, casting, location, and dozens upon dozens of others.

Who should be at the preproduction meeting? Primarily the agency producer, since he or she bears responsibility for every aspect of the production of the commercial. Your producer will likely be joined by the copy/art creative team responsible for creating the commercial at the agency, as well as the agency's business manager, who handles administrative details of the project and oversees the budget. You can also expect one or more representatives from the account-management group.

From the client side, it is mandatory that the Product Manager or advertising manager, or both, be present or represented. If your company has a staff production representative, he or she should be present to help insure production terminology and concerns don't obfuscate the vital communication which must flow back and forth among client, agency, and production company.

The production company should be represented by the project producer; the director *must* attend (a non-negotiable requirement) since he plays such a vital role in the proceedings. The production company may wish to include specialists such as set designers, prop people, stylists, as necessary to the particular job. But it is absolutely essential that the production-company producer and director be present; if they can't be on hand, reschedule the meeting. Don't allow the director to send a surrogate. It's important the director hear you and you hear him—first-hand, and without intermediaries.

When should the preproduction meeting be held? There's no single right answer — instead, the date depends on many considerations, including complexity of the production and availabilities of those who need to attend. One good answer is, not until after the board is fully approved — including all legal and network clearances — and not sooner than a week before shooting is scheduled to start, where that's practical.

I know that preproduction meetings frequently occur as little as two days before shooting commences. If that's the case, I hope you will have anticipated short-scheduling as a problem and scheduled a *pre*-preproduction meeting with client and agency in attendance (if only by conference-call) at which the overall tonality of the commercial, location or set objectives, prop and wardrobe objectives, casting objectives, budget and scene objectives are discussed. This will prevent somebody heading in a wastefully-wrong direction on these very critical elements.

Even if you have had a pre-preproduction meeting with your agency, the actual preproduction meeting should never be scheduled closer to the start of shooting than 48 hours, in order to allow for booking selected talent and to permit some corrective latitude on the last-minute decisions which can contribute mightily to achieving objectives agreed-to in the preproduction meeting.

How should the preproduction meeting be conducted? The simple answer is, by following the agenda laid out in the preproduction-meeting booklet. That booklet, usually prepared by the agency, contains these following items:

● A listing of all client, advertising agency and production-company personnel attending the meeting, with their phone numbers.

● A list of important items to be resolved or confirmed in the course of the preproduction meeting.

● A statement of the overall objective of the advertising, including the tone and look desired. (Suggestion: If your current production is part of a continuing campaign, screen previous executions for the assembled group, and let everyone know what was considered good and not-so-good about those executions.)

● A final, approved script which should be read aloud in the meeting. (Make sure everyone has the *final* version of the copy.)

● The ultimate, approved storyboard itself.

● A list of scene objectives for each scene to be photographed. What's wanted here is a succinct statement of the net visual take-away for the viewer from each scene. Be specific: Saying, "Clearly show the brand name on the package" is a much better scene objective than the less-specific, "Show the package."

● A review of the casting objectives, accompanied by a list of the finalists for each role. Now is your last chance to screen casting tapes, or audition the finalists live, and make final casting decisions. Many clients and agencies do not wait until preproduction to get casting pinned down.

● A checklist to make sure you cover set sketches or location photographs, props, wardrobe, together with the product and packages to be used in each commercial.

● Discussion of demonstrations or product beauty shots. If your commercial has a demonstration, don't neglect to talk about its handling — even if this is the fiftieth time you've filmed it. There are bound to be people involved in the meeting who are unfamiliar with the requirements and subtleties of these very important parts of your advertising. Assuming everyone knows what is wanted is a sure way to get back something in the screening rooms that isn't what you want! Also, make sure your demo is uncompromisingly legal; you don't want embarrassing letters from competitors forcing your shiny new commercial off the air before you've had a chance to utilize it to full effectiveness.

● "The director's discussion." This is the most important part of the preproduction meeting, because it's here the loop is closed, and you find out whether all objectives have been understood, and how they will be incorporated into the commercial. Having heard your objectives and seen the elements you've given him to work with, the director will tell you how he intends to execute the commercial. He is articulating how he

The director must be at preproduction.

133

intends to fulfill your fondest objectives, so listen closely. If you're not clear on precisely how your director plans to deliver what is required, call a halt and *ask questions until you understand*. If you're still not satisfied, stick with the issue; this is the last chance to make sure the director brings back a commercial that will satisfy your objectives. It's important to use the opportunity fully.

● The production schedule. When you start shooting in the morning, as well as when you screen dailies, and receive rough cuts.

● A list of locations or studio addresses. (Hint: A map to locations is very helpful.)

● Production-budget information, such as the production-company AICP form and the agency's own work-order authorization.

● A restatement of agreements on key points and next steps on any open issues. Your agency should issue a call-report summarizing the preproduction meeting. Make sure you read it and agree with it — before shooting starts.

Is it really necessary to go through all that in order to have a good preproduction meeting? The uncompromising answer is, "Yes." A thorough-going preproduction meeting is essential to turning out good advertising. And a good preproduction meeting is a not-unwelcome test of your management and leadership skills: You have to articulate objectives, subscribe others to those goals,

and listen carefully while those others tell you how they're going to practice their arts to achieve the desired effective piece of advertising.

When you watch the screening of your commercial, and everything looks just as you hoped; when it's a fine, strong, healthy baby, you'll be glad you took the time you did in preproduction. There's really no substitute for that time spent.

C H A P T E R   XVI

EIGHT PRODUCTIVE QUESTIONS PRODUCT MANAGERS ARE ALLOWED TO ASK

No one ever said product management was easy. You're trying your best to develop and maintain a good, fruitful relationship with your agency, and keep everyone hard-charging, with enthusiasm levels high. At the same time, you don't want to give away the store financially, or to reveal your own perhaps-modest television experience by appearing to ask "dumb" questions.

This chapter will lay out a list of questions you can ask, which are anything but dumb. (You can start with the axiom that when the person with the money is asking the question, it's always intelligent and perceptive.) As the ultimate buyer of the commercial, you've not only a right but an obligation to be assured about the quality, delivery, professionalism, and price of your productions.

Of them all, price is the area most confusing and random. Over the last 15 years, a number of agencies have dismantled their experienced, autonomous production departments, and turned the television-commercial-buying function over to bright and eager — but frequently inexperienced — agency producers.

If agency commercial buyers are a tad short on experience, however, the vendors of production certainly aren't. They are seasoned, experienced production reps who have been working up estimates for some 20 years now, and know every single comma on the AICP bid sheet.

To begin, therefore, our list of productive questions:

● **Tell me, exactly how much is that going to cost?**
This question should be asked more than any other. You ask it when the

agency gives you the first whisper of an idea for the eventual execution of a commercial. You ask it (absolutely without fail) at the time the board is seriously presented for approval by the agency. You ask it (again, without fail) before you give client approval to the proposed storyboard. And you ask the question without diffidence or hesitation *at every stage of the production process.*

Especially, you ask it whenever someone sidles up to you on the set and murmurs, "Of course this change wasn't in the original plans." When that happens, you're about to encounter an overage; and in our experience the deferral of facing up to overages leads to more agency/client acrimony than almost any other issue. To avoid later argument, make sure the agency attaches a price to any suggestion for a departure from production specifications. You may decide the proposed improvement isn't worth the extra money.

● **How will that work to sell more of my product?**

Why else are you making the commercial, if not to sell product or alter attitudes, or both? This is always a legitimate question to ask during commercial development (an enterprise that's half sales endeavor, half art form). You want to make sure, as entrepreneur's representative, that the Michaelangelos in the creative group don't start regarding the Medici money (i.e., yours) as their very own private bank account. After all, it *is* advertiser money, and you're constrained to see it's optimally invested to achieve a certain defined, strategic, marketing result.

At every stage of the approval and production process — especially when the creatives start waxing rhapsodical about the director or a background musician or the set designer or the wardrobe lady — an acceptable request is, "Help me understand how that's going to sell more of my product." Or, "Help me understand how your recommendation is going to turn around the negative consumer attitudes we discovered in focus groups."

● **Is that the only possible way to accomplish our objective?**

Sure, shooting a scene from a helicopter is exciting, with all the walkie-talkies and attendant technical and logistical fripperies and fascinations.

"But is that the *only* way?" A lot of directors will get the same effect in a large percentage of cases by shooting from a car on an elevated freeway ramp or overpass; or from a church steeple, using a zoom lens; or from a tall building. Using different methods — and lowering cost — the same result can be achieved.

So when your agency arrives, bursting with enthusiasm about how they are going to execute a hideously-expensive production, ask, "Is that the only way to do it?" Followed by the corollary questions, "How many other ways are there?" "What are the advantages of each?" and "What are the attendant cost-differentials?"

You already know the agency is enthusiastically convinced their recommended method is the best way; that's a given. You're not throwing out their recommendation. You simply want to explore options and alternatives so as to make a better-informed decision.

Again, a good agency is capable and resourceful on a dozen different levels. You really can't blame them for having high aspirations on your behalf. If you want to save money, the responsibility for reviewing alternative methods is yours.

● **How do I know that's the right price for the work?**

You don't, and it probably isn't. Over the years, commercial production has developed its own set of ground rules for fattening up estimates to an extent where price often bears no linear or even approximate, relationship to actual cost. You've only to look at the modest scale wages for union crew labor versus charged rates showing up on estimates, to confirm this assertion as fact.

Commercial-production prices in the major production centers have become pretty much what the market will bear. Take two estimates for virtually the same commercial: One is for a large national client; but there's also a carbon-copy storyboard for a regional client. The estimates show a 35-50% differential in production costs. Same commercial, wildly variant costs; and the only difference appears to be the national client's ability to pay more. This is known as the "deep-pocket" school of commercial estimating.

I'm not accusing agencies of profligacy; I commend them, instead, for enthusiasm and high creative aspiration. It's truly important that everyone understand, lofty creative ambition often entails waste. I see variances of 15-30% for producing the same set of production specifications — the primary variable being the sagacity, experience, and aggressiveness of one agency's producers as against the incapability of reaching and standing behind a decision that characterizes another agency's creative team.

There is a correct "Scout's Best Bet" price for every commercial, and it lies somewhere between the lowest amount of money for which the effect can be achieved, and the agency's desiderata estimate. The only way you'll know whether the estimated price is the right price is to go back and ask the third question.

● **Why should I pay overscale? Ever? For anything?**

Some time ago, agency creative folk fell into the habit of paying overscale fees to everybody — hand-models, actresses, kids, dogs, voice-overs. In fact, a certain cachet became attached to paying overscale, with the result that poor old scale players were thought to be dull, uninspired; not at all what a bright, aggressive agency creative team should settle for.

Most union scales provide perfectly adequate compensation for performers; and the offer of an overscale payment is not only unwise and unnecessary, it also undermines the hard work of industry negotiating committees (ANA and AAAA) who hammer out contracts in your behalf with the various talent and labor unions involved in your production.

There are two exceptions to the rule, "Never pay no overscale to nobody." They are:

1. You want to cast an absolutely superb actor or actress for a test-market spot, but your total talent

payments are likely to add up only to basic 13-week scale buyout payments in two markets. In that case, you'll probably have to offer a bonus to attract an outstanding performer. (*Don't* pay "one and a half times" or "two times" scale — it's a dangerous precedent to establish, and one that will come back to haunt you. Pay a flat bonus for signing.)

2. If you want a hand-model who can hit a mark in mid-air, so that a bite of pie (or lipstick or shampoo drop or break-shot) comes into perfect focus for the camera every time, you'll be well advised to go overscale.

A good hand-model earns his or her keep by saving you production time — and, thus, money — on the set. They are so skilled that retakes are almost never necessary.

● **How do the spots planned, as demonstrated by their scene objectives, implement the selling message in my commercial?**

I hold to the pious hope that the agency has provided scene objectives — a fond hope, but not totally idle these days. Then, I'm assuming both you and your agency consider the commercial a vehicle to sell merchandise. It helps when both client and agency understand they are not occupied solely with creating an art form; some cases are expected to move out the front door of the supermarket as a result of their work.

Today's advertising specialists tend to spend inordinate amounts of time and loving attention on executional concerns, as opposed to conceptual selling ideas. We recently heard of an agency producer and director who spent one whole day on location messing around to get the perfect degree and shade of light reflected from a building. Was this to enhance a product shot, you ask? Heaven forefend!

It was, instead, to create ambiance. The product shot received short shrift and barely made the commercial's final cut. Shooting the product wasn't nearly as challenging (or as much fun) as messing around with reflected light.

● **Why do we need specially-commissioned music?**

Today's commercials must come with preprinted "Insert Music Costs Here" blanks at the head of every estimate. It appears we can't begin to produce a commercial without including some form of music — and music costs have shot up like sunflowers, turning eager faces toward the sun of demand.

We seem to have forgotten music has totally pragmatic commercial purposes, as do most other commercial devices. Music can attract the right target audience; or elicit an emotional response from the viewer; or underscore telling points in a selling message; or heighten drama; or serve as a mnemonic enhancer.

If it's performing any three of those functions, music is probably worth some dough. On the other hand, if the music is buried and totally lost — like a rug underfoot at a cocktail party — save your money.

Music under an announcer's track is often money down the tube. If you can hear the music, you're not paying the attention you should to the announcer. The corollary is, why spend money on music that lurks and buzzes behind the advertising copy like a bunch of angry bees about to swarm?

Stock music is available in a number of attractive modes and musical styles, and the cost of stock is a mere pittance. However, when you ask your agency about stock, you might get the genuinely horrified answer I received from one creative group: "We just don't *do* stock!"

Anyone who takes the time to check will find a great many commercials on the air that *do* "do stock" — very well, indeed.

● **Help me understand. Why is that my problem?**

"We ran a couple of hours into overtime."

"The producer couldn't get the lights he wanted, and we had to fly some in."

"The makeup person blew it, and the hair looks ratty."

"The negative was scratched, and we have to reshoot."

You'll hear all of these — and more exotic varieties of the same — as a petition to bathe someone's wounds with the sweet balm of client cash. Your consistent response should be, "Help me understand why that's my problem, and not yours."

If the shoot ran into overtime, is it because (as is most frequently the case) the production company wasn't ready to roll on time in the morning? Then it's their problem, not yours. If the production company neglected to get the right equipment, too bad; again, that's their problem, not yours. You have a right to expect all equipment is working and the assistant cameraman has checked the camera-gate for dirt (hence, no scratched negative). If they didn't call a weather day in time, that's their problem, not yours. If the agency rammed an actor down your throat in casting, same thing.

In short, when you sign off on an estimate for a fixed-bid job — and *you* don't change anything — that's the deal. And any overages? They're *not your problem*; they belong to somebody else.

Don't feel diffident about asking these questions. It's your money, your brand, your campaign, and your career. Any agency worth its salt should be one shake ahead of you — invariably prepared with answers to these questions. Since they have the answers, wouldn't it be a shame for you not to ask the questions?

C H A P T E R XVII

We We Client

Article I

A
CLIENT
BILL
OF
RIGHTS

It used to be fairly simple.

An advertiser would hire an agency, pay 15% or 17.65% commission on billings, and feel reasonably confident of receiving 100% of the loyalty, energy, creativity, and uncompromised fealty of that agency. Clients also had reason to think their agencies would not fool around to any degree with the maintenance of strict competitive sanctity — that is, working for more than one client at a time per product category.

Some change today! The spate of agency and client mergers, the emergence of the mega multi-agency holding company, the loss of distinctive agency "personalities," and the fudging on competitive restraints are severe tests of traditional assumptions that an agency's chief concern and occupation is turning out the best ad-

vertising it can, solely for the benefit of each of its clients.

If the complexities of current advertiser/agency relationships are on your mind — here's a client bill of rights, an enumeration of expectations you're entitled to by the simple fact of being a client, of having hired an advertising agency to be your partner in a marketing venture.

● **A client has the right to expect his agency to be as interested as he is in the primary role of advertising — building share.** Some businesses are, of course, more advertising-driven than others. But most clients expect their advertising to produce a noticeable bottom-line *business* performance. The agency must subscribe to the client's business purposes and goals, and be willing to be measured by its contribution to the business success of its clients. Otherwise, it should pass when asked to take on the new account.

When an agency recommends creative work drawing attention to itself rather than to the client's product — or recommends a course of action contributing mainly to the agency's professional standing among its peers — the client can understandably be excused for wondering if the agency's priorities and his are essentially marching in step.

● **A client has the right to expect his agency to conduct business on his behalf with uncompromising ethical standards.** No expansion of this point should be needed. Yet press stories boil with implications of questionable client-fund use. Many agencies no longer maintain internal staffs of autonomous, professional buyers of production to act as cops on the beat. Often, stewardship of millions of client dollars is turned over to those whose principal interest may be turning out a great job irrespective of production-cost concerns.

A client has a right to expect that his agency's top management has recently reviewed production-buying methods and handling of client funds; and that every one of the agency's departments is managed in a way that would make Caesar's wife look like a slipshod spendthrift.

● **A client has the right to have first-rate, qualified agency personnel assigned to his account.** No trainees or rejects from other accounts, please. It's worth sitting down with your agency's management and discuss-

ing who will be on your business; what their background and experience is; how often you can expect to see them; and how much of the dogsbody work will be delegated to less-experienced lights within the agency account-management and creative teams.

● **A client has the right to expect total fidelity from the people who have asked to handle his business.** Some business relationships have explicit standards by which professional loyalty is measured, such as affidavits and contractual requirements. Most advertisers don't resort to the indignities of conducting closet inventories of agency personnel. There are, however, these valid questions to consider: Do the people working on your business use your product? Are they interested in your business, as opposed to exhibiting a primary interest in selling you their storyboards or print ads? Do they speak well of you and seek to advance your company's cause while cashing payroll checks financed by your account? Do they negotiate aggressively with suppliers in your behalf? *Do they constantly and consistently seek ways to enhance your business through their stated specialty, advertising?*

● **A client has the right to be "sold" by the agency on all recommendations.** There's no implication of "who's boss" in establishing a buyer-seller relationship. Clients welcome a chance to learn, and to appreciate well-thought-out and thoroughly-re-

100% of the creativity, energy, fealty of your agency— a reasonable expectation.

searched agency recommendations. Nothing is so injurious to good client/agency relations or to an advertiser's confidence in his agency, as the desperate suspicion that the agency has not fully explained a recommendation because they haven't thought through their reasoning . . . or, worse, because the recommendation serves some undisclosed agency goal.

● **A client has the right to reject a recommendation or request changes without the agency taking undue offense.** Regardless of how strongly an agency feels the need to lead its client, the success or failure of the advertising is ultimately the client's success or failure — and therefore the client's ultimate responsibility. A truly creative agency has no shortage of advertising solutions to marketing problems; and the fact that a client can't develop enthusiasm for a particular recommendation should not result in a Mexican standoff. Instead, such a failure to agree should turn on the agency's creative juices, so it can demonstrate its professional prowess in devising alternative, equally-attractive advertising solutions.

● **A client has the right to determine how much money is spent on any advertising effort.** Every client has at one time or another been embittered by a project which seemed to take on a life of its own, where budgets ballooned far beyond the boundaries of common sense and reasonable value. It is not only a right but also a responsibility of clients to establish budgets for various purposes; it is the obligation of agencies to honor them, or else challenge them

openly. Subverting or kidding around with established budgets is inexcusable as well as unprofessional.

● **A client has the right to expect that his agency will negotiate vigorously with suppliers.** There is a recent and worrisome situation where some agency creative people appear to act almost as agents and representatives for suppliers rather than their clients. An agent is, by definition, a steward.

Establishing budgets— the client's responsibility; honoring them— the agency's.

Agency people should treat client money as if it were their own. When there's no question of that, there'll be no questions asked afterwards, about agency stewardship.

● **A client has the right to expect that the interlock will look like the storyboard approved.** Yes, of course you want your agency to maintain an eye for creative opportunities all through the production process. On the other hand, agencies have occasionally become so creative during production that the finished commercial bears scant resemblance to the approved storyboard. This is embarrassing at least, and tragic at worst.

In the final analysis, the least the agency must do is, "Shoot the board."

● **A client has the right to expect the agency to feel secure enough to argue.** Advertising is a partnership, with each partner freely contributing particular expertise toward the accomplishment of a shared goal. Partnerships can't exist when there is one dominant partner and one sycophant. If the agency has experience, fact, or evidence refuting the client's position, it is the agency's responsibility to advance those arguments and substantiate them.

On the other hand, the agency that's merely contentious or defends its position solely and endlessly "for creative reasons" is not likely to garner the respect a full partner merits.

Finale

The advertising business is changing — and not always for the better. Clients are cutting commissions (rightly) as agencies' interests appear to lodge more in take-overs that feed the bottom line than in client service. Functions formerly handled by agencies (product naming, package design, media, research, commercial production, promotion) are siphoned off by outside groups, further slashing agency profits. Budgets shrink as advertising effectiveness appears to vanish in a dark cloud of executional excess.

The client-agency partnership can be one of the most exciting and rewarding in business. Advertising is still far and away the preeminent medium for moving products and changing ideas. It is the best way of all to create product preference, distinguishing one product from another.

If the assigned function of advertising is to "help consumers reach a purchasing decision," advertising is absolutely irreplaceable.

All clients need good advertising. This book is intended to help them ask for it with precision and sagacity.

Expectation is a powerful motivator. At the bottom of any success is the expectation of success. The client's principal advertising right is great ideas from the agency. But the client *has to ask* for them; expect the agency to produce them; and learn to approve good ideas when they appear.

Rotten ideas rarely kill great products; but even a breakthrough idea can't make a success of a poor product. Bad executions can't kill good advertising ideas; but elegant executions of "no idea" whistle like the empty wind.

It takes both, just as it takes both client and agency. Furthermore, both must dream . . . and expect and require only the best from the partnership.

Good luck with your dreaming!

Expectation—
a powerful motivator.

I N D E X

Please send me _____ copies of ADVERTISING THAT SELLS at $24.95 each, plus $1.00 for postage and handling.

NAME: _____

ADDRESS: _____

_____

_____

Mail to: Black Rose Publishing Co., Inc.
1420 East McMillan Street
Cincinnati, Ohio 45206

☐ Check or Money Order ☐ Visa ☐ MasterCard

Credit Card #

Exp. date

		/		

_____
Signature

Please send me _____ copies of ADVERTISING THAT SELLS at $24.95 each, plus $1.00 for postage and handling.

NAME: _____

ADDRESS: _____

_____

_____

Mail to: Black Rose Publishing Co., Inc.
1420 East McMillan Street
Cincinnati, Ohio 45206

☐ Check or Money Order ☐ Visa ☐ MasterCard

Credit Card #

Exp. date

		/		

_____
Signature

Please send me _____ copies of ADVERTISING THAT SELLS at $24.95 each, plus $1.00 for postage and handling.

NAME: _____

ADDRESS: _____

_____

_____

☐ Check or Money Order ☐ Visa ☐ MasterCard

Credit Card #

Exp. date

		/		

_____
Signature

Mail to: Black Rose Publishing Co., Inc.
1420 East McMillan Street
Cincinnati, Ohio 45206